510 Essential Words for SSAT & ISEE (Lower/Middle)

With Roots/Synonyms/Antonyms/Usage and more...

By

J. Jonathan

Copyright Notice

All rights reserved. Do not duplicate or redistribute in any form.

Table of Contents

How to increase your vocabulary quickly

Vocabulary is becoming increasingly important for the SSAT/ISEE, and it helps to devote sufficient time to it, as it takes a long time to build an effective vocabulary.

This book contains over 510 Essentials words that appear frequently in the SSAT/ISEE, and uses some of the following techniques to help you remember these words faster and better!

- Word Roots;

Since many English words are derived from Greek & Latin **roots**, it makes sense to be aware of these.

- Prefixes/Suffixes;

Pay attention to the **tone** of the words, whether soft or hard, harsh or mind, negative or positive. This could help you guess when needed.

Prefixes/Suffixes can often help you with identifying the meaning of a word, when in doubt.

- Usage of the Word;

Perhaps the **Best way to increase your vocabulary** is to read, read and read. There is absolutely no substitute for that!

Reading helps you learn new words from the context in which they are used, thereby making it easy to remember the new words and more importantly, how and when they are used.

This book provides you with multiple examples of how a word is used in different contexts.

- Synonyms/Antonyms

Being familiar with related words, increases the number and variety of your **mental associations**.
This helps you retain the meaning of the word more easily.

- Related Words

In order to 'deeply' understand the meaning of a word, it is helpful to study related words at the same time.

e.g. The word **plenty** connotes "sufficient for what is needed" while **abundance** means "more than what is needed".

- Pronunciations

Each word has a pronunciation key that helps you say the word out correctly, thereby aiding retention.

- Practice makes perfect!

Finally, this book has <u>over one thousand exercises</u> to make sure that you remember the meanings of the newly learnt words *'forever'*!

Many ingenious methods, scientifically correct, have been devised to aid the recall of particular facts. These methods are based wholly on the principle that that is most easily recalled which is associated in our minds with the most <u>complex and elaborate groupings</u> of related ideas.

All of the above methods are designed to create a word network in your mind, thereby helping you develop a lasting understanding of the word in the SSAT/ISEE relevant context.

Words with meaning and context

WORD SET 1

abdicate: [ab-di-keyt] Verb
To renounce or give up a throne, right, power, claim, responsibility, or the like, especially in a formal manner.

- The old president of the company decided to **abdicate** his role.
- King Edward VIII **abdicated** his throne to marry the love of his life.

Synonym: forgo, relinquish, renounce, step down, vacate, abandon
Antonym: keep, stay, remain
Further Information
- **Abdicate** is typically used when stepping down from a higher position of power in an organization, institution, or a country.
- Originated from the Latin word *ab + dicates* meaning "away, from" + "declare."
- Can be confused with **abnegate (verb)** which means to deny or renounce something.

aberration: [ab-uh-REY-shuh n] Noun
Deviation from what is normal, expected, or usual; Departure from truth, morality, etc.
An irregularity from the normal.

- Mary's sudden outburst was an **aberration** from her calm demeanor.
- If a person can roll his tongue, he is thought to have a genetic **aberration**.

Synonym: oddity, peculiarity, quirk, eccentricity, strangeness
Antonym: normality
Further Information
- Originated from the Latin word *ab + errare* meaning "away from" + "to stray."
- **Aberration** can also mean a temporary mental irregularity or disorder.
- In Astronomy, an **aberration (of light)** is the appearance of a heavenly body in a position different from its actual or true location in space due to Earth's movement.

abhorrent: [ab-HAWR-uh nt] Adjective
Causing or deserving strong dislike or hatred. Feeling or showing strong dislike or hatred.

- John's **abhorrent** behavior caused him to get kicked out of the cafe.
- He woke up due to the **abhorrent** noise made by the passing train.

Synonym: disgusting, despicable, loathsome, repulsive, detestable, repugnant
Antonym: admirable
Further Information
- Originated from *ab + horrere* meaning "away from" + "to shudder."
- The synonym **repugnant** implies a stronger meaning of disgust and aversion.

abide: [uh-BAHYD] Verb
To act in accordance with rules.
To endure without yielding.

- The students must **abide** by the rules of the school or get punished.
- I said I would **abide** by their decision and follow them.

Synonym: comply with, obey, follow, adhere to
Antonym: disallow, avoid, contradict
<u>Further Information</u>
- Commonly used in the phrase **abide by** meaning "to put up with or tolerate."
- Originated from the Old English *a + bidan* or *gebidan* meaning "remain, wait, or delay."
- The phrases "submit to," "stand for," and "put up with" have the same meaning as **abide**.
- Might be confused with **abode (noun)** which means "a place where a person lives."

abrasive: [uh-BREY-siv] Noun/Adjective
Any material or substance used for grinding, polishing, etc. (n.)
Causing damage, wear, or removal of surface material by grinding or rubbing. (adj.)
Causing irritation, annoy, or ill will. (adj.)

- The athlete was banned from playing future games for using **abrasive** language. (adj.)
- The carpenter is using an **abrasive** to smoothen the furniture. (n.)

Synonym: annoying, caustic, nasty, irritating, rough
Antonym: agreeable, calm, kind, mild, pleasant
<u>Further Information</u>
- Originated from the Latin word *ab + radere* meaning "away, from" + "to scrape."
- Its synonym **irritating** denotes a stronger connotation: "causing annoyance or pain."

abstain: [ab-STEYN] Verb
To hold oneself back voluntarily, especially from something regarded as improper or unhealthy.
To choose not to do or have something.

- If you want to live healthy, you should **abstain** from drinking too much soda.
- Marcus found it difficult to **abstain** from sleeping during the movie.

Synonym: desist, forgo, pass up, quit, refrain
Antonym: continue, do, accept
<u>Further Information</u>
- **Abstain** also refers to "to refrain from casting one's vote" as in during an election.
- Originated from the French word *abstenir* meaning "to withhold oneself."

abundance: [uh-BUHN-duh ns] Noun
An extremely plentiful or over-sufficient quantity or supply.
An ample quantity.

- New York City is a metropolis with an **abundance** of high rise buildings.
- There is an **abundance** of fruits in the forest.

Synonym: affluence, bounty, myriad, plenty, plethora
Antonym: few, lack, little, scarcity
Further Information
- **Abundant** is the adjective form of **abundance**.
- Related to the French word *abundance* and originated from the Latin word *abundantia* meaning "fullness, plenty."
- The word **plenty** connotes "sufficient enough to supply need" while **abundance** means "more than what is needed or in excess."

abysmal: [uh-BIZ-muh l] Adjective
Extremely poor or bad.
Immeasurably low or deep, as in like an abyss.

- Since Marc played video games the whole week, he earned an **abysmal** score on the test.
- The number of audience attending the concert was **abysmal** and way lower than their expectations.

Synonym: appalling, dreadful, awful, terrible, frightful, atrocious
Antonym: hopeful, good, outstanding
Further Information
- The word was first recorded in mid 1600s combining **abysm (an abyss) + -al**.
- A related adjective is **abyssal** which means "unfathomable" or "relating to the bottom of ocean depths."

accredited: [uh-KRED-i-tid] Adjective/Verb
Officially recognized as meeting the essential requirements, as of academic excellence. (adj.)
To give official authorization to or approval of. (v.)

- The charity is **accredited** by the government and officially allowed to raise funds. (v.)
- Jonathan is working hard to become an **accredited** teacher. (adj.)

Synonym: authorised, certified, vouched for, credited
Antonym: unauthorised, unofficial
Further Information
- **Accredited** is typically used to refer to a recognized educational institution that maintains a certain standard of qualification.
- It can also mean "recognized as outstanding," for example, "He is an accredited scientist."

activism: [AK-tuh-viz-uh m] Noun
A practice that emphasizes direct vigorous action especially in support of or opposition to one side of a controversial issue.
Consists of efforts to promote, impede, or direct social, political, economic, or environmental reform with the desire to make improvements in society.

- Hunger strike is a form of **activism** that was used by Mahatma Gandhi.
- Participating in discussions and debates is an important part of **activism.**

Synonym: advocacy, involvement, militancy
Antonym: none
Further Information
- The plural word **Movements** is related to **activism** which means "actions or activities by a group of people with the same advocacy."
- Originated from the German word *Aktivismus* first recorded in 1905.

admire: [ad-MAHYUR] Verb
To regard with wonder, pleasure, or approval.
To feel respect and approval for (someone or something).

- I **admire** his perseverance in finishing his studies despite working two jobs.
- One can just **admire** the beauty of nature on a nice spring day and momentarily forget all troubles.

Synonym: adore, appreciate, cherish, idolize, marvel at, revere
Antonym: condemn, despise, denounce
Further Information
- To **admire** a person is to "hold someone in high regard."
- Originated from the late 1500s' Latin word *admirari* meaning "to wonder at."
- The synonym **adore** implies a stronger meaning: "to worship."

admonish: [ad-MON-ish] Verb
To urge to a duty.
To reprove or scold, especially in a mild and good-willed manner.

- The teacher **admonished** him for forgetting his homework at home.
- I **admonished** him to eat healthier and exercise more.

Synonym: advise, berate, censure, scold, reprimand
Antonym: allow, compliment, flatter
Further Information
- While **reprimand** is a synonym, it implies severe and formal warning.
- **Berate** also denotes a stronger meaning: "to scold vehemently."
- Originated from the Middle English words *amonesche, admonesse,* and *amoness.*

REVIEW EXERCISE 1

Match the word with its synonym.

___	1.	abdicate	a.	despicable
___	2.	aberration	b.	forgo
___	3.	abhorrent	c.	terrible
___	4.	abide	d.	vacate
___	5.	abrasive	e.	rough
___	6.	abstain	f.	peculiarity
___	7.	abundance	g.	movement
___	8.	abysmal	h.	scold
___	9.	accredited	i.	appreciate
___	10.	activism	j.	authorized
___	11.	admire	k.	plenty
___	12.	admonish	l.	obey

From the words above, fill in the blanks with the most appropriate word. The word form may need changing.

1. He is _____ for being a talented athlete and a student leader.

2. The carpenter uses an _____ pad to polish a newly made furniture.

3. He was fined by the traffic officer for failing to _____ by the rules of the road.

4. When a king _____ his position, it creates a political tension all across the country.

5. The sudden increase of crime in the area is an _____ to the otherwise relatively clean record of the local government.

6. Environmental _____ helps people understand current issues concerning the environment and encourages them to take action.

7. Do not go home too late or Dad will _____ you. You'll be grounded!

8. Many people find war to be morally _____ and detrimental to the human race.

9. An _____ food inspector visited the restaurant and gave it a high score because of its cleanliness.

10. The _____ of flowers in the area makes it a perfect place for a bee colony.

11. Johnny needs to _____ from strenuous activities to fully recover from his knee injury.

12. His boss reminded him that he needs to improve his _____ performance before the end of the year.

WORD SET 2

adroit: [uh-DROIT] Adjective
Expert or nimble in the use of the hands or body.

- He is proving to be an **adroit** doctor who has saved many lives.
- You have to be an **adroit** soccer player to qualify for the team.

Synonym: skillful, resourceful, ingenious, dexterous
Antonym: clumsy
Further Information
- From the mid-17th French phrase *à droit* meaning "on the" + "according to right."
- The related term **dexterous** is almost an exact synonym, meaning: "skillful in the use of hands or body."

affable: [af-uh-buh l] Adjective
Pleasantly easy to approach and to talk to.
Showing warmth and friendliness.

- John is a popular boy with an affable smile.
- We need an **affable** salesperson to increase the number of customers.

Synonym: personable, warm, friendly, amiable, cordial
Antonym: unfriendly, disagreeable, impolite
Further Information
- Originated from the Latin word *ad + fari* meaning "to" + "speak."
- **Affable** implies being open to conversations while its synonym **polite** implies agreeable manner in general.

affirm: [uh-FURM] Verb
To state or assert positively.
To express agreement with or commitment to.

- Singing the team anthem **affirms** one's loyalty to their sports team.
- The museum curator cannot **affirm** which of the paintings is genuine.

Synonym: assert, confirm, declare, guarantee, agree
Antonym: deny, forget, veto
Further Information
- Originated from the Latin word *ad + firmus* which means "to" + "strong."
- The synonym **assert** implies a stronger meaning of confidence or agreement.
- In Law, **affirm** means "to state something solemnly before a court or magistrate, but without an oath."

affluent: [AF-loo-uh nt] Adjective/Noun
Having an abundance of wealth, property, or other material goods. (adj.)
A rich person. (n.)

- He desires a more **affluent** lifestyle and is willing to work hard for it. (adj.)
- The high-end restaurant attracts **affluent** customers especially on weekends. (n.)

Synonym: moneyed, prosperous, rich, upscale, well-off
Antonym: destitute, failing, poor
Further Information
- From the Latin word *ad* + *fluere* meaning "to" + "flow."
- An older usage of **affluent** means "a stream or river that flows into a larger stream."
- Do not confuse with **effluent** which means waste liquid.

aggregate: [AG-ri-git] Noun/Adjective/Verb
Formed by the conjunction or collection of particulars into a whole mass or sum. (adj.)
A sum, mass, or assemblage of particulars. (n.)
To bring together; collect into one sum, mass, or body. (v.)

- This **aggregate** rock is made up of various minerals and elements. (adj.)
- This group is an **aggregate** of students from different districts. (n.)
- The samples collected in the swamp should be **aggregated** in the laboratory. (v.)

Synonym: cumulative, combined, accumulated
Antonym: individual, uncombined, particular
Further Information
- Originated from the Latin word *ad* + *grex/greg* meaning "toward" + "a flock."
- **Aggregate** is commonly used in science to describe small samples or elements being combined, specifically in Geology.

ailment: [eyl-muh nt] Noun
A physical disorder or illness, especially of a minor or chronic nature.

- She is suffering from a rare **ailment** and several medicines have been ineffective.
- The doctor is quite good at curing common **ailments.**

Synonym: ache, sickness, disease, disorder, illness, malady
Antonym: health
Further Information
- It is a two-part word **ail + ment. Ail** is from an old English word *eglan* meaning "to trouble or plague." **-ment** is a suffix from the Latin *-mentum* which is added to words to imply "as a result of a certain action."

alternate: [AWL-ter-neyt] Verb/ Adjective/Noun
To interchange repeatedly and regularly with one another in time or place. (v.)
Being in a constant state of succession or rotation; Constituting an alternative. (adj.)
A person authorized to fill the position, exercise the duties, etc., of another who is temporarily absent. (n.)

- You have to **alternate** with your brother in mowing the lawn. (v.)
- Create an **alternate** email for your social media accounts so your school email's inbox is not flooded with notifications. (adj.)
- The **alternate** teacher is liked by the students and the faculty. (n.)

Synonym: backup, substitute, surrogate, interchange, double, stand-in
Antonym: primary, noncyclic
Further Information
- The verb and adjective form evolved in the 1500s from the Latin *alternus* meaning "one after the other."
- Related to the word **alternative** which means "giving a limited number of options."

amass: [uh-MASS] Verb
To gather for oneself.
To collect into a mass or pile.

- My father loved comic books and **amassed** a great number of them in his collection.
- **Amassing** a large number of followers on Twitter is difficult.

Synonym: assemble, collect, compile, garner, hoard
Antonym: disperse, divide, scatter, separate
Further Information
- Originated from the Latin word *massa* which means "lump."
- The synonym **hoard** implies collecting a large amount of something valuable that needs to be guarded.

amenable: [uh-MEE-nuh-buh l] Adjective
Ready or willing to answer, act, agree, or yield.
Open to influence, persuasion, or advice.

- Some leaders like **amenable** team members in order to avoid conflict in the team.
- He was an easy going child and **amenable** to change.

Synonym: agreeable, responsive, susceptible
Antonym: unsusceptible
Further Information
- Originated from the French phrase *à + mener* meaning "to" + "lead."
- **Credulous** could be mistaken as a synonym of amenable, but it means naïve or gullible.

ancestral: [an-SES-truh l] Adjective
Descending or claimed from ancestors/forefathers.
Serving as a forerunner, prototype, or inspiration.

- Our family's **ancestral** home needs to be regularly maintained and renovated.
- Having blue eyes is an **ancestral** trait which dates back to my great-great-grandfather.

Synonym: familial, genealogical
Antonym: none
Further Information
- **Ancestral** evolved from the Latin word *ante + cedere* which means "before" + "to go."
- Ancestor (n.) should not be confused with ***descendant*** which means successor or offspring.

annotate: [AN-uh-teyt] Verb
To supply with critical or explanatory notes.
To comment upon in notes.

- It is quite challenging to **annotate** the works of Shakespeare.
- You are free to **annotate** the textbooks with supplemental notes.

Synonym: comment, commentate, construe, define, elucidate
Antonym: confuse, mystify, obscure
Further Information
- Originated from the Latin word *ad + nota* meaning "to" + "a mark."
- **Annotate** is slightly different from **comment**, as the latter implies a casual "remark or observation."

anomaly: [uh-NOM-uh-lee] Noun
A deviation from the common rule, type, arrangement, or form.
An odd, peculiar, or strange condition, situation, quality, etc.

- Kevin's calm and quiet demeanor is an **anomaly** in this noisy class.
- An **anomaly** in the results of the laboratory tests caused the experiment to be halted.

Synonym: aberration, abnormality, deviation, inconsistency, irregularity, oddity
Antonym: conformity, normality, regularity, standard
Further Information
- Originated from the Greek noun *anomalos* which is rooted in the word compound *an + homalos* meaning "not" + "even."
- Its synonym **aberration** implies an "error or deviation" from the norm.

REVIEW EXERCISE 2

Match the word with its synonym.

___	1.	adroit	a.	malady
___	2.	affable	b.	skillful
___	3.	affirm	c.	agreeable
___	4.	affluent	d.	friendly
___	5.	aggregate	e.	cumulative
___	6.	ailment	f.	familial
___	7.	alternate	g.	confirm
___	8.	amass	h.	prosperous
___	9.	amenable	i.	aberration
___	10.	ancestral	j.	comment
___	11.	annotate	k.	collect
___	12.	anomaly	l.	substitute

From the words above, fill in the blanks with the most appropriate word. The word form may need changing.

1. The_____ family owns multiple companies and properties around town.

2. Cancer is a serious _____ which a lot of doctors are concerned about.

3. She is considered an_____artist with several exhibitions to her credit.

4. He arrived at the beautiful_____ house passed down from his great grandma.

5. Can you_____ different samples for the experiment?

6. I hope the supervisor is_____ to new ideas.

7. Today, an_____ coach will be conducting the training and workshop.

8. He_____ that his statements are true and that he's always honest.

9. During his days, Grandpa_____ different awards from his charitable works.

10. Having different colored eyes is considered an_____.

11. This book should be_____ by an expert.

12. Sam is quite_____ that's why everybody likes him.

WORD SET 3

apathetic: [ap-uh-THET-ik] Adjective
Having or showing little or no emotion.
Not interested or concerned.

- His **apathetic** behavior did not go over well with his manager, and he was fired.
- The boy showed an **apathetic** attitude towards his homework.

Synonym: callous, indifferent, laid-back, passive, stoic, uninterested
Antonym: caring, compassionate, concerned, feeling, interested
Further Information
- Originated from the Greek word *a* + *pathos* meaning "without" + "emotion or feeling."
- Evolved from apathy + pathetic.

apex: [ap-eks] Noun
The tip, point, or vertex.
At the point of climax or peak.

- His time as the president of the company is the **apex** of his career.
- They reached the **apex** of the mountain around noon and set up camp.

Synonym: apogee, climax, culmination, pinnacle, peak
Antonym: base, bottom
Further Information
- **Apex** remains relatively unchanged from its Latin root word *apex* meaning "summit, tip, or top."
- The synonyms **climax** and **culmination** typically refer to abstracts and ideas such as "climax of the movie" and not a location.

appalling: [uh-PAW-ling] Adjective
Causing dismay or horror.

- He was dismissed because of his **appalling** actions and inexcusable behavior.
- The **appalling** crime was reported all over the world.

Synonym: alarming, ghastly, astounding, awful, dire, disheartening, shocking
Antonym: calming, comforting, delightful, good
Further Information
- Originated from the French word *a* + *palir* meaning "to" + "grow pale."
- **Appalling** implies a stronger emotion than **astounding** or **awful**.

apparent: [uh-PAR-uh nt] Adjective
Capable of being easily perceived or understood.
Seemingly real or true, but not necessarily so.

- It was **apparent** by the look on his face that he was the winner of the national lottery.
- The results from his examination are pretty **apparent** and show that he is in good health.

Synonym: evident, plain, obvious, seemingly, superficial
Antonym: unclear, obscure, genuine
Further Information
- Originated from the Latin word *apparere* which means "appear or to come in sight."
- It can also mean as "being entitled to a right of inheritance such as property, throne, etc.," as in **heir apparent.**

appreciable: [uh-PREE-shee-uh-buh l] Adjective
Sufficient to be readily perceived or estimated.

- There is an **appreciable** difference in doing just enough and going the extra mile.
- She has to work harder because of her **appreciable** learning issues.

Synonym: definite, detectable, discernible, marked, noticeable, considerable, substantial, sizeable
Antonym: ambiguous, imperceptible, indistinct
Further Information
- Originated from the Late Latin word *ad + pretium* meaning "to" + "price" or "to rise in value."
- **Appreciable** is used when something is tangible, quantifiable, or obvious.
- May be confused with **appreciative** which means to show gratitude.

apprehensive: [ap-ri-HEN-siv] Adjective
Uneasy or fearful about something that might happen.

- The captain was **apprehensive** for the safety of the firefighters during the fire.
- After a lot of practice, she was less **apprehensive** of her ability to ride a bicycle.

Synonym: afraid, concerned, doubtful, jittery, jumpy
Antonym: calm, certain, clear, collected, composed
Further Information
- Originated from Latin word *ad + "prehendre"* meaning "to" + "seize."
- The word **apprehend** has similar roots but means to arrest someone, or to understand a concept.

arbitrary: [AHR-bi-trer-ee] Adjective
Subject to individual will or judgment without restriction.
Based on a random choice or personal whim rather than any reason or system.

- An **arbitrary** behavior is not healthy among friends and can create tension.
- It was an **arbitrary** decision to pardon him of his offenses.

Synonym: capricious, discretionary, erratic, frivolous, inconsistent
Antonym: consistent, definite, dependable, logical
Further Information
- Originated from the Latin word *arbiter* meaning "judge, supreme ruler."
- In Mathematics, **arbitrary** means "(of a constant or other quantity) of unspecified value."

aromatic: [ar-uh-MAT-ik] Adjective/Noun
Having a distinctive and pleasant smell. (adj.)
A plant, drug or medicine yielding a fragrant smell. (n.)

- The garden is quite **aromatic** during spring and summer. (adj.)
- Her **aromatics** help her relax when she is doing yoga. (n.)

Synonym: fragrant, perfumed, pungent, savoury, scented
Antonym: bland, dull, flavorless
Further Information
- Originated from the Greek word *aromatikos* (a form of the word aroma) which means "giving out an aroma or sweet smell."
- In Chemistry, **aromatic** means "of or relating to specific organic compounds."

arrogant: [AR-uh-guh nt] Adjective
Making claims or pretensions to superior importance or rights.
Characterized by or proceeding from sense of superiority, self-importance, or entitlement.

- Drew's **arrogant** behavior is the result of her being ridiculously rich.
- His **arrogant** claims were found to be false during the investigation.

Synonym: bossy, cocky, haughty, pompous, pretentious, smug, conceited, proud
Antonym: humble, modest, shy, timid
Further Information
- Originated from the Latin word *ad + rogare* meaning "to" + "ask or entreat."
- **Arrogant** is often linked to aggressive and loud behavior.

articulate: [ahr-TIK-yuh-lit] Adjective/ Verb
Expressed clearly in distinct syllables. (adj.)
To utter clearly and distinctly. (verb)

- His **articulate** speech won many hearts and minds. (adj.)
- The teacher carefully **articulated** the project instruction. (v.)

Synonym: coherent, eloquent, expressive, fluent, well-spoken
Antonym: inarticulate, hesitant, unintelligible
Further Information
- Originated from the Latin word *articulus* (diminutive form of *artus,* "a joint") which means "to be a part of."
- **Articulate** usually describes a person who can speak well, usually with charisma and charm.

artillery: [ahr-TIL-uh-ree] Noun
Mounted projectile-firing guns or missile launchers.
The troops or the branch of an army concerned with the use and service of such weapons.

- The army's advanced **artillery** won them the war.
- The attacking **artillery** is quite intimidating to the enemies.

Synonym: battery, cannon, gunnery
Antonym: none
Further Information
- Its definite origin is the Old French word *artillier* meaning "to provide with engines of war."
- Also attributed to Latin *articulum* "joint," Latin *apere* "to attach," or Old French *atillier* "to equip."

ascendant: [uh-SEN-duh nt] Adjective
Moving upwards or rising in power or influence.

- The **ascendant** political party is winning all elections.
- The King desperately looked for ways to defeat the **ascendant** enemy.

Synonym: predominant, rising, dominant, superior
Antonym: humble, inferior
Further Information
- Originated from the Latin word *ad + scandere* meaning "to" + "climb."
- It can also be spelled as **ascendent.**
- In astrology, **ascendant** means "the point on the ecliptic at which it intersects the eastern horizon at a particular time, typically that of a person's birth."

REVIEW EXERCISE 3

Match the word with its synonym.

___	1.	apathetic	a.	fragrant
___	2.	apex	b.	eloquent
___	3.	appalling	c.	concerned
___	4.	apparent	d.	erratic
___	5.	appreciable	e.	cannon
___	6.	apprehensive	f.	sizeable
___	7.	arbitrary	g.	alarming
___	8.	aromatic	h.	indifferent
___	9.	arrogant	i.	evident
___	10.	articulate	j.	rising
___	11.	artillery	k.	climax
___	12.	ascendant	l.	haughty

From the words above, fill in the blanks with the most appropriate word. The word form may need changing.

1. Because he shows off his achievements, many people think he's _____.

2. Lavender has an _____ fragrance which many people love.

3. George was _____ about getting a tattoo and piercing.

4. His speech showed that he is _____ and charming.

5. The soldiers are trying to evade the large _____ that destroyed their infantry.

6. The_____ accident was witnessed by many.

7. The boss was_____ to the hard work of his team.

8. Lisa needs to study more to see an_____ improvement in her scores.

9. His promotion is the_____ of his career.

10. John the actor was considered_____ talent and had many offers to choose from.

11. The tired judge laid down an_____ decision during the hearing.

12. The solution was_____ after many hours of brainstorming.

WORD SET 4

assess: [uh-SES] Verb
To fix or determine the amount of (damages, a tax, a fine, value etc.).
To estimate officially the value of (property, income, etc.) as a basis for taxation.

- Tom's house is being **assessed** so he can put it up on the market.
- The damage from the fire was **assessed** at 400,000 dollars.

Synonym: appraise, check, determine, estimate, evaluate
Antonym: none
Further Information
- Originated from the Latin word *ad + sedere* meaning "to" + "sit."
- **Assess** is to determine a value while **evaluate** implies observation and measurement.

assimilate: [uh-SIM-uh-leyt] Verb
To take in and understand fully.
To absorb and digest.

- Children need to be able to **assimilate** new ideas.
- She had to **assimilate** a lot of information on her first day of class.

Synonym: comprehend, grasp, incorporate, understand
Antonym: exclude, misinterpret, mistake, misunderstand
Further Information
- Originated from Latin *ad + similis* meaning "to" + "like."
- **Assimilate** implies combination of new information and facts into what you already know.

astound: [uh-STOUND] Verb
To overwhelm with amazement.
Shock with wonder or surprise.

- The librarian was **astounded** by the number of books missing from the shelves.
- He was **astounded** by the awesome present from his mother.

Synonym: astonish, bewilder, confound, confuse, dumbfound
Antonym: calm, clarify
Further Information
- The original Vulgar Latin *extonare* evolved into the early form of the word in Middle English *astouned* or *astoned*.
- **Astound** means "general surprise" while **bewilder** and **confound** imply "surprise and confusion."

astute: [uh-STOOT] Adjective
Having insight or shrewdness.

- Dr. Washington is an **astute** member of the faculty and an award-winning researcher.
- The investigator's **astute** observation solved the case quickly.

Synonym: canny, intelligent, keen, clever, crafty
Antonym: foolish, idiotic, inept, naïve
Further Information
- From the Latin word *astus* meaning "craft."
- **Astute** implies "expertise in a field" while **crafty** means "clever at achieving one's aims by indirect or deceitful methods."

augment: [awg-MENT] Verb
To make larger; enlarge in size, number, strength, or extent.

- His fortune is **augmented** by the success of his business.
- The plan is to **augment** our current solution to solve the root cause of the problem.

Synonym: amplify, boost, enhance, enlarge, expand
Antonym: compress, condense, contract, decrease
Further Information
- From the Latin word *augere* meaning "to increase."
- In Linguistics, **augment** means "a vowel prefixed to past tenses of verbs in Greek and other Indo-European languages."

austerity: [aw-ster-i-tee] Noun
Severity/harshness of manner, life, etc.
Difficult economic conditions caused by reduced government spending.

- The spendthrift man did not believe in **austerity**.
- The **austerity** measures taken by the government make the lives of the people more difficult.

Synonym: severity, harshness, frugality, strictness
Antonym: informality, kindness, mildness
Further Information
- Originated from the Latin word *austerus* meaning "severe."
- Its root **austere** means "harsh and rigid."

avid: [AV-id] Adjective
Showing great enthusiasm for or interest in.

- She is an **avid** comic book collector who regularly attends comic conventions.
- The actor ensured that he made time for his **avid** fans.

Synonym: enthusiastic, ardent, keen, devoted
Antonym: indifferent, apathetic, reluctant
<u>Further Information</u>
- From the Latin word *avere* meaning "to crave."
- The word **obsess** is related to **avid**, but the former implies "extreme dedication and interest."

awe: [aw] Noun/Verb
An overwhelming feeling of reverence, admiration, fear, etc., produced by that which is grand, sublime, extremely powerful, or the like. (n.)
To inspire with reverence or dread. (v.)

- Jessica is in **awe** of the places she visited during her European trip. (n.)
- She's **awed** by the fact that she is meeting her music idol. (v.)

Synonym: admiration, apprehension, astonishment, dread
Antonym: disregard, apathy
<u>Further Information</u>
- Originated from the evolution of the Old English *ege* which means "terror or dread" and Old Norse *agi* meaning "fright."
- Related to but not similar to **awestruck** which means "horrified or very surprised."

barometer: [buh-ROM-i-ter] Noun
Scientific instrument that measures atmospheric pressure.
Anything that indicates changes.

- A new **barometer** is essential for accurate weather prediction.
- The quizzes are a good **barometer** of improvements in scholastic performance.

Synonym: weatherglass
Antonym: none
<u>Further Information</u>
- Originated from the combination of the Greek word *baros* meaning "weight" and the English word *-meter.*
- **Barometer** can also mean "something that measures or identifies."

belated: [bih-LEY-tid] Adjective
Coming or being after the customary, useful, or expected time.
Late, delayed, or detained.

- **Belated** birthday greetings are still very much appreciated and enjoyed.
- We started the discussion without the **belated** participant because our timeline is hectic.

Synonym: delayed, late, overdue, tardy
Antonym: early, on time, punctual
Further Information
- Originated from the English *be + late* which means delayed.
- In 16th century, **belated** meant "overtaken by the night."

bellow: [BEL-oh] Verb/Noun
To emit a hollow, loud, animal cry, as from a bull or cow. (v.)
An act or sound of bellowing. (n.)

- Her **bellowing** startled the entire auditorium and alarmed everyone. (v.)
- The cow's **bellow** was loud enough to be terrifying and made the kids cry. (n.)

Synonym: roar, yell, shout, holler, scream
Antonym: whimper, whisper
Further Information
- Evolved from the Old English word *bylagan* meaning "to sound or roar."
- **Bellow** is louder than a **scream** or a **yell**.

benevolent: [buh-NEV-uh-luh nt] Adjective
Characterized by or expressing goodwill or kindly feelings.
Intended for benefits rather than profit.

- Mary was attracted to the **benevolent** attitude of the group.
- The school received generous gifts from the **benevolent** alumni.

Synonym: benign, caring, compassionate, generous, humane
Antonym: cruel, hateful, mean, merciless

REVIEW EXERCISE 4

Match the word with its synonym.

___	1. assess	a.	benign
___	2. assimilate	b.	astonish
___	3. astound	c.	late
___	4. astute	d.	admiration
___	5. augment	e.	roar
___	6. austerity	f.	amplify
___	7. avid	g.	appraise
___	8. awe	h.	devoted
___	9. barometer	i.	weatherglass
___	10. belated	j.	incorporate
___	11. bellow	k.	clever
___	12. benevolent	l.	frugality

From the words above, fill in the blanks with the most appropriate word. The word form may need changing.

1. The _____ birthday party was quite an event and came as a big surprise to him.

2. A _____ is used by meteorologist to predict the weather.

3. It is difficult to _____ all the new concepts I learned in the advanced class.

4. He is in _____ of the places he visited and the people he met.

5. The teacher will _____ your presentation today.

6. People have to live through years of _____ after experiencing war.

7. She was _____ by the performance of the actors.

8. The king was _____ to friends but cruel to enemies.

9. The small business _____ the family income.

10. He needs to have an _____ observation when collecting data.

11. Ginny is an _____ collector of dolls, especially Barbie.

12. The crowd's _____ was really loud during the concert.

WORD SET 5

berth: [burth] Noun
A ship's allocated place at a wharf or dock.
A bed or bunk in a vessel or train, usually narrow and fixed to a wall.

- It was a sad goodbye for the sailors when the ship left its **berth**.
- She suffers from seasickness and keeps to her **berth**.

Synonym: dock, port, wharf, bed
Antonym: none
<u>Further Information</u>
- Originated from the English word *bear + th* meaning "adequate sea room."
- **Berth** may also mean "a job or position."
- A popular idiom **give a wide berth to** means "to stay away from or steer clear."

bilingual: [bahy-LING-gwuhl] Adjective/Noun
Able to speak two languages with the expertise of a native speaker. (adj.)
A bilingual person. (n.)

- Miko grew up in a **bilingual** community which speaks English and Japanese. (adj.)
- Being able to speak fluent English and Japanese, she is considered **bilingual.** (n.)

Synonym: polyglot
Antonym: none
<u>Further Information</u>
- From the Latin word *bi + lingua* meaning "having two" + "tongue."
- A person who can speak several languages is called **multilingual** or **polyglot.**

billiards: [BIL-yerdz] Noun
Any of several games played with hard balls of ivory or of a similar material that are driven with a cue on a cloth-covered table enclosed by a raised rim of rubber, especially a game played with a cue ball and two object balls on a table without pockets.

- He is getting better at playing **billiards**, and he's planning on joining competitions.
- **Billiards** is a type of mental sport which requires strategy and planning.

Synonym: pool, snooker
Antonym: none
<u>Further Information</u>
- Evolved from the French word *bille* meaning "stick of wood" and Medieval Latin *billia* meaning "tree trunk."
- While usually interchangeable, **pool** is a smaller table game.

bolster: [BOHL-ster] Noun/Verb
A long, often cylindrical, cushion or pillow for a bed, sofa, etc; something that helps support weight. (n.)
To add to, support, or uphold. (v.)

- The wooden skeleton of the new house needs more **bolsters** for safety. (n.)
- A good compliment **bolstered** her confidence. (v.)

Synonym: help, aid, boost, buttress, cushion
Antonym: block, decrease, halt, hinder
Further Information
- Evolved from Old Norse *bolstr*, Danish, Swedish, and Dutch *bolster* which means "to swell."
- A more common synonym is **support.**

boon: [boon] Noun/Adjective
Something to be thankful for; a benefit or blessing for which one should be grateful. (n.)

- A generous donation to the orphanage is a huge **boon** for the kids.
- The new train will be a **boon** to many travelers.

Synonym: advantage, blessing, windfall, godsend, jolly
Antonym: bad fortune, bad luck, disadvantage
Further Information
- Originated from Old French word *bon* meaning "good."
- An older usage of **boon** means "a favor or request."

brooch: [brohch] Noun
A clasp or ornament having a pin at the back for passing through clothing and a catch for securing the point of the pin.

- Mina lost the new **brooch** she bought last week for her birthday.
- She values the **brooch** worn by the women of her family.

Synonym: jewelry, breastpin
Antonym: none
Further Information
- Evolved from the Latin words *broochus* or *broocus* meaning "projecting."
- **Brooch** should not be confused with **broach** which means "to mention or suggest for the first time."

bystander: [BAHY-stan-der] Noun
A person present but not involved.

- A **bystander** witnessed the car accident yesterday and gave his statement to the police.
- Thankfully, no **bystander** was hurt during the stampede in the concert.

Synonym: onlooker, eyewitness, observer, passerby
Antonym: participant
Further Information
- First recorded in the early 1600s as combination of *by + stand + er* meaning "near" + "stand" + designation of person.
- The **bystander effect** is a social psychological phenomenon in which individuals are less likely to offer help to a victim when other people are present. Related to **apathy**.

cacophony: [kuh-KOF-uh-nee] Noun
Harsh discordance of sound.
A discordant and meaningless mixture of sounds.

- The **cacophony** of the city makes one miss the countryside.
- The teacher's thoughts were interrupted by the **cacophony** of students.

Synonym: noise, discord, harshness
Antonym: euphony
Further Information
- From the Greek work *kakos + phone* meaning "bad" + "sound."
- The direct antonym of **cacophony** is **euphony** meaning "pleasant agreeable sound."

callous: [KAL-uh s] Adjective/Noun
Made hard; To be insensitive. (adj.)
Hardened part of skin. (n.)

- They have a **callous** attitude towards the plight of the victims. (adj.)
- Wearing leather shoes without the right socks will result in **callous** on your feet. (n.).

Synonym: apathetic, careless, uncaring, hard, heartless
Antonym: caring, compassionate, concern, feeling
Further Information
- Originated from the Latin word *callus* or *callum* meaning "thick skin."
- **Callous** is a variant spelling of **callus** which means "a thickened and hardened part of the skin or soft tissue, especially in an area that has been subjected to friction."

caricature: [KAR-i-kuh-cher] Noun
A picture, description, etc., ludicrously exaggerating the peculiarities or defects of persons or things.

- She commissioned a **caricature** of her dog from an amazing artist.
- The newspaper's article made a **caricature** of the current state of the government.

Synonym: cartoon, farce, parody, satire
Antonym: flattery, praise, seriousness
Further Information
- Originated from the Vulgar Latin word *carricare* meaning "to load a wagon or cart."
- **Caricatures** are often seen in art, while **satire** is commonly seen in literature.

caustic: [KAW-stik] Adjective
Capable of burning, corroding, or destroying living tissue.
Severely critical or sarcastic.

- You have to wear gloves during chemistry lab because we'll be using **caustic** substances.
- Her **caustic** remark shows her abrasive nature and rude attitude.

Synonym: abrasive, acerbic, acidic, biting
Antonym: bland, kind, mild, nice
Further Information
- Originated from Greek word *kaiein* meaning "to burn."
- A **caustic** attitude is much worse than **abrasive** behavior.

cavity: [KAV-i-tee] Noun
A hollow place.
A hollow space or a pit in a tooth, most commonly produced by tooth disease.

- The mole burrowed a hollow **cavity** in the garden and made it home.
- I need to visit the dentist to have my **cavity** filled and make sure my teeth are healthy.

Synonym: crater, aperture, gap, orifice
Antonym: bulge
Further Information
- From the Latin word *cavus* meaning "hollow."
- A **cavity** implies "an enclosed empty space" while a **hole** is "an opening or a gap."

REVIEW EXERCISE 5

Match the word with its synonym.

___	1.	berth	a.	onlooker
___	2.	bilingual	b.	uncaring
___	3.	billiards	c.	pool
___	4.	bolster	d.	bunk bed
___	5.	boon	e.	abrasive
___	6.	brooch	f.	noise
___	7.	bystander	g.	windfall
___	8.	cacophony	h.	aid
___	9.	callous	i.	breastpin
___	10.	caricature	j.	cartoon
___	11.	caustic	k.	crater
___	12.	cavity	l.	polyglot

From the words above, fill in the blanks with the most appropriate word. The word form may need changing.

1. He's glad to have a big _____ in the boat so he can rest comfortably.

2. His _____ behavior is disliked by many and that's why he doesn't have friends.

3. John's _____ jokes offend many of his colleagues.

4. The _____ fits well with her style and overall attire.

5. A _____ table is usually colored green and made with felt cloth.

6. The workshop will help _____ his career and boost his confidence.

7. Jenny's _____ looks quite funny and quirky.

8. Donations are a huge _____ for the charity and the people it helps.

9. The _____ of the students in the gym was loud and rowdy.

10. The _____ just stared during the emergency and did nothing.

11. There's a large _____ in the mountain which is closed to outsiders.

12. _____ can speak two distinct languages.

WORD SET 6

cede: [seed] Verb
To yield or formally surrender to another.

- The infantry **ceded** the previously occupied territory in order to regroup.
- In 1867, Russia **ceded** Alaska to the US.

Synonym: capitulate, concede, give in, give up, grant
Antonym: fight, hold, keep, refuse
Further Information
- Originated from the French word *ceder* and the Latin word *ceded* meaning "to yield."
- The phrase **give in** implies "surrender to an ongoing and continuous pressure."

celebrated: [SEL-uh-brey-tid] Adjective
To be renowned or well-known.

- A **celebrated** actor was given an Oscar for the first time in years.
- This book is a collection of poems by **celebrated** authors and prominent people.

Synonym: acclaimed, revered, great, glorious
Antonym: unexalted, inglorious, obscure
Further Information
- Originated from the Latin word *celeber/celebr* meaning "frequented or honored."
- The synonym **acclaimed** implies "a publicly acknowledged excellence" whereas **celebrated** implies "being popular."
- Celebrated is the past tense of **celebrate** which means to "party/salute/observe etc."

cellar: [SEL-er] Noun
A room or set of rooms, for the storage of food, fuel, etc., wholly or partly underground and usually beneath a building.

- The teenagers discovered a secret **cellar** full of books and paintings.
- The restaurant owner wanted a wine **cellar** built in his restaurant.

Synonym: basement, vault, apartment
Antonym: attic
Further Information
- Originated from the Late Latin word *cella* meaning "storeroom or chamber."
- The synonym **vault** implies "arched enclosed space, typically large."

chalet: [sha-LEY] Noun
A kind of farmhouse, low and with wide eaves, common in Alpine regions.
Any cottage, house, ski lodge, etc.

- The princess wanted an exclusive **chalet** for her annual ski vacation.
- We got lost locating the **chalet** due to the snowstorm in the mountains.

Synonym: cabin, hut, house
Antonym: none
Further Information
- Evolved from the Latin *casa* meaning "house."
- A **chalet** is a type of cabin, usually in snowy regions, typically Swiss-style.

chastise: [chas-TAHYZ] Verb
To discipline, especially by corporal punishment.
To criticize severely.

- She was **chastised** for something that was not even her fault.
- The teacher chose to give constructive criticism rather than **chastise.**

Synonym: berate, castigate, flog, punish, upbraid
Antonym: compliment, laud, praise
Further Information
- Originated from the Old French *chastieer* meaning "to punish."
- Should not be confused with **chaste** which means "innocent" or "moral/modest."

chronic: [KRON-ik] Adjective
Continuing for a long time or recurring frequently.
Having long had a disease, habit, weakness, or the like.

- The manager gave a final warning to the employee who was a **chronic** late comer.
- Her **chronic** headache makes life harder for her.

Synonym: constant, continual, continuous, habitual
Antonym: acute
Further Information
- Originated from the Greek word *khronos* meaning "time."
- **Chronic** is typically used to describe diseases with prolonged or continued symptoms, often severe.

clamor: [KLAM-er] Noun/Verb
A loud uproar, as from a crowd of people; a vehement expression of desire or dissatisfaction. (n.)
To utter noisily. (v.)

- The **clamor** from the crowd alerted the police officers that something was wrong. (n.)
- They **clamored** for their ideas during the team meeting and argued a lot. (v.)

Synonym: noise, brouhaha, buzz, hubbub, noise
Antonym: calm, order, peace
Further Information
- Originated from the Latin word *clamare* meaning "to cry out."
- Spelled as **clamour** in British English.

clandestine: [klan-DES-tin] Adjective
Characterized by, done in, or executed with secrecy or concealment, especially for purposes
of subversion or deception.

- The superheroes were on a **clandestine** mission to save the world.
- Their **clandestine** meeting went unnoticed for quite some time.

Synonym: covert, fraudulent, furtive, hidden, illicit
Antonym: authorized, honest, known
Further Information
- Originated from the Latin word *clam* meaning "secretly."
- **Clandestine** is often used to describe actions and events while **hidden** is generally used for objects and people.

cleft: [kleft] Noun
A space or opening made by two parts of a body.
A hollow area or indentation.

- A chin with a **cleft** is believed to be quite rare, just like blue eyes.
- They discovered a large **cleft** between the two mountains.

Synonym: crack, clove, crack, gap
Antonym: connected, fixed, whole
Further Information
- Originated from the Old High German and Danish *kluft* meaning "a split."
- A **cleft palate** is a medical condition where the mouth is not well-formed during birth.

coalesce: [koh-uh-LES] Verb
To grow together or into one body.
To unite so as to form one mass, community, etc.

- During New Year's Eve, the community **coalesces** in the town square to celebrate together.
- Good ideas usually **coalesce** into a strong theory used in research.

Synonym: consolidate, fuse, integrate, unite, adhere, combine
Antonym: divide, separate
Further Information
- Originated from the Latin word *cum + alere* meaning "with" + "nourish."
- **Coalesce** implies "natural and gradual formation into a bigger body" while **consolidate** implies "to bring together into a unified whole."

coddle: [KOD-l] Verb
To treat tenderly; Nurse or tend indulgently.
To cook (eggs, fruit, etc.) in water that is just below the boiling point.

- Mothers typically **coddle** their children when they're sick or under the weather.
- A perfect poached egg is usually **coddled** in water with a bit of vinegar.

Synonym: baby, indulge, pamper
Antonym: ignore, neglect
Further Information
- Originated from the Latin word *calidus* meaning "warm."
- Not to be confused with the word **cuddle** which means "to hold close in an affectionate manner."

cohabit: [koh-HAB-it] Verb
To live together as if married, usually without legal or religious sanction.
To dwell with another or share the same place, as different species of animals.

- **Cohabiting** usually brings up new challenges for people.
- Zoologists often observe different animals **cohabiting** harmoniously.

Synonym: conjugate, couple, mingle, coexist
Antonym: disjoin
Further Information
- Originated from the Latin *co + habitare* meaning "together" + "dwell."
- **Coexist** is a more common synonym of **cohabit**.

REVIEW EXERCISE 6

Match the word with its synonym.

___	1. cede	a.	basement
___	2. celebrated	b.	continuous
___	3. cellars	c.	revered
___	4. chalet	d.	concede
___	5. chastise	e.	coexist
___	6. chronic	f.	combine
___	7. clamor	g.	castigate
___	8. clandestine	h.	hubbub
___	9. cleft	i.	crack
___	10. coalesce	j.	indulge
___	11. coddle	k.	cabin
___	12. cohabit	l.	covert

From the words above, fill in the blanks with the most appropriate word. The word form may need changing.

1. The house has a wine _____with many varieties of vintage wines.

2. Mom _____ my brother for eating too much candy.

3. The professor is also a _____ scientist popular among his peers.

4. The crowd _____ in the auditorium for the announcement.

5. When babies are upset, _____ by their mothers helps soothe them.

6. Spies often go on _____ operations and secret missions.

7. It is usually difficult to _____ with strangers in one house.

8. My _____ headache will not go away and it's driving me crazy.

9. Young customers _____ to buy the discounted video games.

10. The family bought a huge _____ in the Alps for vacations during winter.

11. A _____ is often found between two mountains.

12. The soldiers _____ territory when they lost the battle.

WORD SET 7

coherence: [koh-HEER-uhns] Noun
Quality of being logical and consistent.

- Legal contracts should have very high **coherence** and clarity.
- Editing your written work is important for **coherence.**

Synonym: consistency, continuity, integrity, rationality, solidarity
Antonym: difference, disagreement, discord
<u>Further Information</u>
- Originated from the Latin word *com + haerare* which means "together" + "to adhere, stick."
- **Coherence** implies clarity of textual or written work.

coil: [koil] Verb/Noun
To wind into continuous, regularly spaced rings, one above the other. (v.)
A connected series of spirals or rings into which a rope or the like is wound. (n.)

- To create a weak electromagnet, **coil** a copper wire around a stick. (v.)
- There was a **coil** missing inside the machine; that's why it's not working. (n.)

Synonym: wind, loop, twist, curl
Antonym: line
<u>Further Information</u>
- Originated from Latin word *com + legere* meaning "together" + "to gather."
- The verb usage of **coil** implies "slow, twisting movement."

collude: [kuh-LOOD] Verb
To act together through a secret understanding, especially with evil or harmful intent.
To conspire in a fraud.

- There's a rumour that the captain **colluded** with the other team to lose the game.
- The criminals **colluded** together to hide from the police.

Synonym: connive, conspire, plot, scheme
Antonym: none
<u>Further Information</u>
- Originated from the Latin word *col + ludere* meaning "together" + "to play."
- **Collude** is commonly misspelled as **colude** which is not a word.

commerce: [KOM-ers] Noun
An interchange of goods or commodities, especially on a large scale between different countries (foreign commerce) or between different parts of the same country (domestic commerce).

- E-**commerce** involves selling and buying of goods and services online.
- Most of the country's **commerce** revolves around oil exports.

Synonym: business, economics, exchange, industry, trade
Antonym: none
Further Information
- Originated from Latin word *com + merx/merc* meaning "together" + "merchandise."
- **Commerce** implies "a group of business, customers, and other entities acting together to form economic exchange" while **business** implies "an occupation, profession, or trade."

complacent: [kuh m-PLEY-suh nt] Adjective
Pleased, especially with oneself or one's merits, advantages, situation, etc., often without awareness of some potential danger or defect.

- The government officials are too **complacent** to change old policies.
- The sailors' **complacent** attitude sank the ship and caused the demise of the passengers.

Synonym: self-satisfied, pleased, satisfied, self righteous, smug
Antonym: unhappy, unsure
Further Information
- Originated from the Latin word *complacere* meaning "be very pleasing."
- **Complacent** has a negative connotation as in being smug while **confident** or **contented** evoke positive emotions.

complement: [KOM-pluh-muh nt] Noun/ Verb
Something that completes or makes perfect. (n.)
To complete; form a complement to. (v.)

- A good salary is a **complement** to a happy career, but fulfilment is important. (n.)
- The black dress **complements** her smooth skin and striking blue eyes. (v.)

Synonym: accompaniment, addition, aggregate, augmentation
Antonym: none
Further Information
- Originated from the Latin word *complere* meaning "fill up."
- Not to be confused with **compliment** which means an expression of praise, commendation, or admiration."

compliant: [kuh m-PLAHY-uh nt] Adjective
Obeying, obliging, or yielding, especially in a submissive way.
Manufactured or produced in accordance with a specified body of rules.

- His **compliant** nature makes him vulnerable at times.
- The product is **compliant** with the latest standards.

Synonym: docile, flexible, willing, obedient
Antonym: inflexible, obstinate, stubborn, unyielding
Further Information
- Evolved in the 1600s from the word *com + plere* meaning "with, together" + "to fill."
- Not to be confused with **complaint** which means "to express dissatisfaction."

composed: [kuh m-POHZD] Adjective
To be calm, tranquil or serene.

- A **composed** leader during a project helps the team focus and solve problems.
- Johnny's **composed** attitude is common among Marines and military personnel.

Synonym: calm, collected, confident, poised, serene.
Antonym: agitated, nervous, upset
Further Information
- Originated from the Old French word *com + poser* meaning "with, together" + "to place."
- Related to **compose** which is a verb and means "create/comprise/calm down."

compromise: [KOM-pruh-mahyz] Noun/Verb
A settlement of differences by mutual concessions; an agreement reached by adjustment of conflicting or opposing claims, principles, etc., by reciprocal modification of demands. (n.)
To expose or make vulnerable to danger, suspicion, scandal, etc. (v.)

- A **compromise** was reached by the two parties to resolve the conflict. (n.)
- James needs to **compromise** with the budget committee in order for the project to proceed.

Synonym: accommodation, accord, adjustment, bargain, concession
Antonym: denial, disagreement, refusal
Further Information
- Originated from the Latin word *com + promittere* meaning "with, together" + "to release, let go."
- A **compromise** is often misspelled as **compremise** which is not a word.

conceited: [kuh n-SEE-tid] Adjective
Having an excessively favorable opinion of one's abilities, appearance, etc.

- He's a little **conceited**; that's why he does not have many friends.
- Jonah's **conceited** attitude is a hurdle to his improvements.

Synonym: egotistical, arrogant, cocky, vain, proud
Antonym: diffident, humble, meek
Further Information
- Originated from the late 14th century word *conceiven* meaning "something formed in the mind, thought, notion."
- **Conceited** implies "being too proud of one self or an excess of self-confidence."

concise: [kuh n-SAHYS] Adjective
Expressing or covering much in few words; brief in form but comprehensive in scope.

- Can you make this contract a bit more **concise** and clear?
- The most effective speech is usually **concise** and direct.

Synonym: short, pithy, succinct, terse, abridged
Antonym: lengthy, long-winded, wordy
Further Information
- Originated from the Latin word *con + caedere* meaning "completely" + "to cut."
- **Concise, succinct,** and **terse** usually refers to "speech or writing using few words."

concoct: [kon-KOKT] Verb
To prepare or make by combining ingredients, especially in cookery.
To devise or to make up.

- She was able to **concoct** a delicious dinner in a very short time.
- You have to **concoct** a plan to solve our current problem and deal with future issues.

Synonym: formulate, contrive, devise, discover
Antonym: demolish, destroy, ruin
Further Information
- Originated from the Latin *com + coquere* meaning "together" + "to cook."
- Its noun form **concoction** means "a mixture of various ingredients or elements."

REVIEW EXERCISE 7

Match the word with its synonym.

___	1.	coherence	a.	arrogant
___	2.	coil	b.	short
___	3.	collude	c.	calm
___	4.	commerce	d.	obedient
___	5.	complacent	e.	twist
___	6.	complement	f.	smug
___	7.	compliant	g.	accommodation
___	8.	composed	h.	rationality
___	9.	compromise	i.	formulate
___	10.	conceited	j.	business
___	11.	concise	k.	addition
___	12.	concoct	l.	connive

From the words above, fill in the blanks with the most appropriate word. The word form may need changing.

1. She _____ the loose thread around her finger.

2. The enemies _____ to fool everyone.

3. The country's _____ has been going down due to the corrupt government.

4. His _____ attitude made everyone think he's lazy.

5. This black shirt will _____ my pants and shoes.

6. The business processes are _____ with international standards.

7. Jimmy is usually cool and _____ in the face of emergency.

8. In every conflict, _____ is a good solution.

9. He likes to always talk about himself because he is _____.

10. Make sure your questions are _____ because we don't have much time.

11. The witch _____ a magical brew.

12. The explanation still has no _____ and is very confusing.

WORD SET 8

concur: [kuh n-kur] Verb
To agree.
To coincide.

- Does the team **concur** with the leader's statement and plan of action?
- Their wedding **concurred** with the holidays and they celebrated both occasions.

Synonym: agree, approve, coincide, jibe, accede
Antonym: clash, disagree
<u>Further Information</u>
- Originated from the Latin word *con + currere* meaning "together with" + "to run."
- The synonym **approve** implies a stronger agreement than **concur.**

condolence: [kuh n-DOH-luh ns] Noun
Expression of sympathy with a person who is suffering from sorrow, misfortune, or grief.

- It is okay to offer **condolences** to someone who is grieving.
- A sincere expression of **condolences** helps someone deal with difficult situations.

Synonym: sympathy, compassion, consolation, solace, comfort
Antonym: none
<u>Further Information</u>
- Originated from the Late Latin word *com + dolere* meaning "with, together" + "to grieve."
- The word **condolement** is a lesser known synonym of **condolence.**

confectionery: [kuh n-FEK-shuh-ner-ee] Noun
Sweets and chocolates considered collectively.
A confectioner's shop.

- He likes all kinds of **confectionery** including candies, cakes, and milkshakes.
- The **confectionery** along Main Street sells the most amazing chocolate cakes.

Synonym: bakery, pastry shop, sweets, candy
Antonym: none
<u>Further Information</u>
- Evolved from the Classical Latin word *com + facere* meaning "with" + "to make, to do."
- A **bakery** usually sells bread and other pastries while a **confectionery** focuses on sweets.

confront: [kuh n-FRUHNT] Verb
To face in hostility or defiance.
To present for acknowledgment, contradiction, etc.

- To **confront** your issues is a brave act and essential to being an adult.
- The team **confronted** the urgent problems first.

Synonym: challenge, accost, defy, encounter, meet
Antonym: avoid, dodge, evade
Further Information
- Originated from the Latin word *con + frons* meaning "with" + "face."
- **To confront someone** implies "facing something/someone to accuse or criticize."

congestion: [kuh n-JES-chuh n] Noun
Overcrowding, especially in a small area.
An excessive or abnormal accumulation of blood or other fluid in a body part or blood vessel.

- No one likes being stuck in a severe traffic **congestion**.
- The doctors will begin treating her pulmonary **congestion**.

Synonym: blockage, bottleneck, overpopulation, crowding
Antonym: lack
Further Information
- Originated from the Latin word *con + gerere* meaning "together" + "bring."
- **Congestion** is sometimes misspelled as **conjestion** which is not a word.

conscientious: [kon-shee-EN-shuh s] Adjective
Controlled by or done according to one's inner sense of what is right.
Careful and painstaking.

- The people want a **conscientious** government.
- Her designs are very **conscientious** and evoke deep emotions.

Synonym: thorough, careful, diligent, painstaking, meticulous
Antonym: careless, indifferent, uncritical
Further Information
- Originated from the Latin word *com + scire* meaning "with/thoroughly" + "to know."
- **Conscientious** Implies "more attention to detail" compared to **careful.**

consent: [kuh n-SENT] Verb/Noun
To permit, approve, or agree; comply or yield. (v.)
Agreement in sentiment, opinion, a course of action, etc. (n.)

- She **consented** to their request and allowed them to visit her villa. (v.)
- Can you email me Sarah's **consent** so we can process the papers? (n.)

Synonym: agreement, concession, approval, assent, authorization
Antonym: denial, disagreement, disapproval, dissent
Further Information
- Originated from the Latin with *con + sentire* meaning "together" + "feel."
- **Consent** implies "giving permission or approval" while **agree** is to "go along with."

consolidate: [kuh n-SOL-i-deyt] Verb
To bring together (separate parts) into a single or unified whole.
To unite or combine.

- The executives decided to **consolidate** their companies into one large enterprise.
- The librarian **consolidated** the book collection.

Synonym: combine, make firm, cement, centralize, concentrate
Antonym: decrease, discourage, disperse, dissuade
Further Information
- Originated from the Latin word *solidus* meaning "solid."
- **Consolidated** is the adjective form of the word as in "consolidated document."

conspiracy: [kuh n-SPIR-uh-see] Noun
An evil, unlawful, treacherous, or surreptitious plan formulated in secret by two or more persons.
A combination of persons for a secret, unlawful, or evil purpose.

- Many **conspiracy** theories are simply not true.
- The government always tries to protect itself from **conspiracies.**

Synonym: collusion, plot, scheme, sedition, treason
Antonym: faithfulness, honesty, ignorance
Further Information
- Originated from the Latin word *conspirare* meaning "agree, plot."
- **Conspiracy** is a formal term used in politics, civil law, and criminal law.

contemporary: [kuh n-TEM-puh-rer-ee] Adjective/Noun
Of the present time. (adj.)
A person belonging to the same time or period with another or others. (n.)

- There is an exhibit of **contemporary** art in the plaza. (adj.)
- His **contemporaries** are very critical of his work. (n.)

Synonym: modern, new, present-day, current, latest
Antonym: future, old
Further Information
- Originated from the Medieval Latin word *con + tempus* meaning "together with" + "time."
- **Modern** art is those created between the 1860s to 1960s. Any art after that is considered **contemporary**.

contemptible: [kuh n-TEMP-tuh-buh l] Adjective
Deserving of or held in contempt.

- **Contemptible** actions are punishable by law and can get you in jail.
- It was **contemptible** of the employee to embarrass his boss in front of everyone.

Synonym: despicable, shameful, abhorrent, abominable, disgusting
Antonym: delightful, kind, likeable, lovable
Further Information
- Originated from the Latin word *com + temnere* meaning "together" + "to slight or scorn."
- **Contemptible** is often misspelled as **contemptable** which is not a word.

contentious: [kuh n-TEN-shuh s] Adjective
Tending to argument or strife.
Causing, involving, or characterized by argument or controversy.

- Sarah's **contentious** attitude is a hindrance to the team's improvement.
- We should always handle **contentious** situations with poise.

Synonym: quarrelsome, antagonistic, combative, testy
Antonym: agreeable
Further Information
- Originated from the Latin word *com + tendere* meaning "with, together" + "to stretch."
- **Contentious** implies stronger negative feelings compared to **debatable.**

REVIEW EXERCISE 8

Match the word with its synonym.

___	1.	concur	a.	combine
___	2.	condolence	b.	modern
___	3.	confectionery	c.	approval
___	4.	confront	d.	blockage
___	5.	congestion	e.	scheme
___	6.	conscientious	f.	sympathy
___	7.	consent	g.	shameful
___	8.	consolidate	h.	agree
___	9.	conspiracy	i.	sweets
___	10.	contemporary	j.	combative
___	11.	contemptible	k.	scrupulous
___	12.	contentious	l.	challenge

From the words above, fill in the blanks with the most appropriate word. The word form may need changing.

1. He was a _____ person who took his duties very seriously.

2. There is a traffic _____ on the highway because of the accident.

3. Ben's _____ deed is punishable by the law and frowned upon by society.

4. Sometimes it is difficult to _____ your fears and get over them.

5. He _____ to have his blood taken for tests for the health check.

6. All manufacturing activities have been _____ in the new premises.

7. Please accept my _____ on your loss.

8. I _____ with your proposal and would like to go ahead with the deal.

9. Tracy's _____ attitude puts off many people.

10. The _____ bridge was the first ever to connect the two islands.

11. Do not listen to _____ theories which are illogical.

12. The _____ around the corner sells gummy bears.

WORD SET 9

contrary: [KON-trer-ee] Adjective/Noun
Opposite in nature or character. (adj.)
Something that is the opposite. (n.)

- **Contrary** to popular belief, being a celebrity is difficult and requires a lot of work. (adj.)
- Although he was down, he did not give up; on the **contrary**, he fought harder. (n.)

Synonym: antagonistic, adverse, conflicting, contradictory, discordant
Antonym: agreeable, consistent, friendly
Further Information
- Originated from the Latin word *contra* meaning "against."
- The synonym **hostile** evokes a stronger negative emotion.

contrived: [kuh n-TRAHYVD] Adjective
Obviously planned or forced.

- Everybody knew that was a **contrived** story which was fake.
- The movie plot seems **contrived** and boring.

Synonym: false, phony, overly planned
Antonym: genuine, real
Further Information
- Originated from the Medieval Latin word *contropare* meaning "compare."
- **Contrived** implies artificial.

convene: [kuh n-VEEN] Verb
To come together or assemble, usually for some public purpose.

- The participants are **convening** in the auditorium.
- In case of an emergency, all students and faculty should calmly **convene** in the open field.

Synonym: meet, assemble, gather, summon
Antonym: disperse, divide
Further Information
- Originated from the Latin word *con + venire* meaning "together" + "come."
- **Convene** implies "a gathering with a purpose as a group" while **summon** is "to call people to attend."

convent: [KON-vent] Noun
A community of persons devoted to religious life under a superior.
The building or buildings occupied by such a society.

- The **convent** is more than 300 years old and needs an immediate renovation.
- The city ordered a renovation of the historic **convent**.

Synonym: nunnery, abbey, cloister
Antonym: none
Further Information
- Evolved from the Middle French word *com + venire* meaning "together" + "to come."
- Modern use of **convent** implies a community or building for nuns, while **monastery** is for monks.

conversant: [kuh n-VUR-suh nt] Adjective
Familiar with, by use or study.

- Living in an English-speaking community will make you **conversant** with the English language faster.
- He is very **conversant** with medieval history.

Synonym: experienced, abreast, acquainted, knowledgeable, practiced
Antonym: ignorant, inexperienced
Further Information
- Originated from the Latin word *com + vertere* meaning "with, together" + "to turn."
- **Conversant** implies a certain expertise in a field or topic.
- Usually followed by "with."

convey: [kuh n-VEY] Verb
To carry, bring, or take from one place to another.
To communicate.

- In olden times, horses were used to **convey** water from rivers to villages.
- Make sure that you **convey** your message clearly and directly.

Synonym: transport, bring, send, transfer, transmit
Antonym: receive, take
Further Information
- Originated from the Medieval Latin word *con + via* meaning "together" + "way."
- **Convey** commonly refers to speech while **express** refers to emotions.

convivial: [kuh n-VIV-ee-uh l] Adjective
To be friendly.
Of or befitting a feast.

- Jamie is a **convivial** wedding host who appeals to his audience.
- I was so happy that my new classmates are **convivial** and friendly.

Synonym: fun-loving, cheerful, clubby, festive, genial
Antonym: apathetic, depressed, gloomy, lethargic
<u>Further Information</u>
- Originated from the Latin word *con + vivere* meaning "with" + "live."
- **Convivial** implies cheerfulness in general which **friendly** implies easiness to connect with others.

cope: [kohp] Verb
To struggle or deal with, especially on fairly even terms or with some degree of success.
To face and deal with responsibilities, problems, or difficulties, especially successfully or in a calm or adequate manner.

- Manny believes he can **cope** with any hurdles and problems along the way.
- After having a serious illness, he could not **cope** with living alone anymore.

Synonym: manage, contend, confront, endure, grapple
Antonym: hold, keep, refuse
<u>Further Information</u>
- Originated from the Greek work *kolaphos* meaning "blow with the fist."
- **Cope** is sometimes confused with **coup** which is short for the phrase *Coup d'état* which means "the illegal and overt seizure of a state by the military or other elites within the state apparatus."

copious: [KOH-pee-uh s] Adjective
Large in quantity or number.
Having or yielding an abundant supply.

- She ordered a **copious** amount of food and drinks for the party.
- The farmers are hoping for a **copious** harvest this year.

Synonym: abundant, ample, extensive
Antonym: lacking, meager
<u>Further Information</u>
- Evolved from the Latin word *copia* meaning "plenty." Another word with the same root is **cornucopia** which is a noun meaning "abundant supply."
- An older usage of **copious** means "profuse in speech or ideas."

cordial: [KAWR-dee-uh l] Adjective
Courteous and gracious.
Warm and friendly.

- Countries maintain a **cordial** relationship to keep international peace.
- Her **cordial** personality brings many guests to the restaurant.

Synonym: friendly, affectionate, amicable, cheerful, cosy
Antonym: cold, cool, disagreeable, insincere
Further Information
- Originated from the Latin word *cor* meaning "heart..
- While it implies friendliness, **cordial** can also be used in negative way, as in "cordial dislike."

corroborate: [kuh-ROB-uh-reyt] Verb
To make more certain.
To confirm.

- The witness **corroborated** the accident that happened on 10th Street.
- My manager can **corroborate** the fact that I accomplished all my tasks today.

Synonym: authenticate, confirm, justify, substantiate, validate
Antonym: disprove, invalidate, veto
Further Information
- Evolved from the Latin word *robur* meaning "strength."
- **Corroborate** is typically used in legal situations to confirm the authenticity of certain information.

counter: [KOUN-ter] Noun/Adjective
A table or display case on which goods can be shown, business transacted, etc. (n.)
An opposite. (adj.)

- Proceed to the **counter** on the left if you want to process your application. (n.)
- His **counter** proposal is not enough to convince the committee. (adj.)

Synonym: opposing, contrasting, different, table, worktop
Antonym: agreeing, harmonious

REVIEW EXERCISE 9

Match the word with its synonym.

___	1. contrary	a.	confirm
___	2. contrived	b.	transfer
___	3. convene	c.	worktop
___	4. convent	d.	manage
___	5. conversant	e.	contradictory
___	6. convey	f.	cheerful
___	7. convivial	g.	abundant
___	8. cope	h.	assemble
___	9. copious	i.	abbey
___	10. cordial	j.	phony
___	11. corroborate	k.	experienced
___	12. counter	l.	affectionate

From the words above, fill in the blanks with the most appropriate word. The word form may need changing.

1. The host was very _____ during the party and welcomed everyone personally.

2. The books' plot is too _____ to be real.

3. He is _____ with a variety of computer languages.

4. _____ with difficult situations is necessary for survival.

5. The _____ is a historical religious site.

6. _____ to popular belief, setting-up a business is quite easy.

7. The evidence _____ his claims and statements.

8. He forgot his car keys on the kitchen _____ .

9. It is difficult to _____ complicated thoughts in such a short time.

10. Beth is liked by everyone because she is relaxed and _____.

11. There is a _____ amount of food in the pantry.

12. Companies _____ together to work on the global project.

WORD SET 10

courier: [KUR-ee-er] Noun
A messenger, usually traveling in haste, bearing urgent news, important reports or packages, diplomatic messages, etc.
Any means of carrying news, messages, etc., regularly.

- The **courier** is very efficient in delivering packages and mail.
- We don't have a **courier** nearby; you may need to drive downtown.

Synonym: messenger, bearer, carrier, dispatcher, emissary
Antonym: receiver
Further Information
- Evolved from the Italian word *corriere* meaning "to run."
- Should not be confused with the word **carrier** which means "a person or thing that carries."

craft: [kraft] Noun/Verb
An art, trade, or occupation requiring special skill. (n.)
To make or manufacture (an object, objects, product, etc.) with skill and careful attention to detail. (v.)

- Honing your **craft** takes years of training and practice. (n.)
- **Crafting** a beautiful design digitally is very challenging. (v.)

Synonym: expertise, art, technique
Antonym: clumsiness, ignorance, inability
Further Information
- Originated from Old English word *cræft* meaning "power, physical strength."
- **Craft** implies "skills in manual talent or trade" while **hobby** is "an activity done to pass the time."

craven: [KREY-vuh n] Adjective/Noun
Cowardly. (adj.)
A coward. (n.)

- He sometimes has the tendency to be **craven** when faced with big problems. (adj.)
- Everybody thought Jimmy is a **craven** until he saved a little girl from the burning building. (n.)

Synonym: weak, timid
Antonym: bold, brave
Further Information
- Originated from the Latin word *crepare* meaning "to crack or creak."
- **Craven** is not related to the word **crave** which means "to want desperately."

crease: [krees] Noun/Verb
A ridge or groove produced by folding, heat, pressure, etc. (n.)
To make a crease or creases in or on. (v.)

- Create a **crease** by folding the paper diagonally. (n.)
- Don't **crease** the gift wrapper yet before you use it. (v.)

Synonym: fold, wrinkle, bend, bulge, cockle
Antonym: none
Further Information
- Altered from the 1600s' word *creaste* meaning "a ridge."
- Not related to the word **crest** which means "the highest part of anything."

creche: [kresh] Noun
A representation of a nativity scene.
A place where small children can be left to be looked after while their parents are doing something else.

- A **creche** is being set up a month before December in front of the church.
- Johnny likes staying at the **creche** when I'm at work.

Synonym: nursery, playroom, preschool
Antonym: none
Further Information
- Originated from the Old French *cresche* meaning "a crib, manger, or stall."
- **Crib** is another synonym for **creche.**

credulous: [KREJ-uh-luh s] Adjective
Willing to believe or trust too readily, especially without proper or adequate evidence.

- People should avoid being **credulous** during elections and do their research carefully.
- My **credulous** son believes that I am Batman and he is Robin.

Synonym: gullible, naive, accepting, believing, dupable
Antonym: skeptical, suspecting, suspicious
Further Information
- Originated from the Latin word *credere* meaning "to believe."
- Being **credulous** implies "ignoring available facts or evidence."

crevice: [KREV-is] Noun
A crack forming an opening.

- Do not go playing too far or you'll fall into a **crevice.**
- The cleaning staff makes sure that all **crevices** of the hotel are clean.

Synonym: crack, gap, abyss, chasm, chink
Antonym: none
Further Information
- Originated from the Latin word *crepare* meaning "to rattle, crack."
- **Crevice** is a variant spelling of **crevasse** which has a similar meaning.

crude: [krood] Adjective/Noun
In a raw or unprepared state. (adj.)
Crude oil. (n.)

- Submit your essay even in its **crude** draft so I can help you edit. (adj.)
- A delivery of **crude** will arrive later for the factory machines. (n.)

Synonym: vulgar, boorish, unpolished, cheap, coarse
Antonym: clean, decent, delicate, polished, pure
Further Information
- Originated from the Latin word *crudus* meaning "rough, uncooked."
- The word **uncouth** can also be used as a synonym when referring to behavior or manner, as in "**uncouth** person."

culminate: [KUHL-muh-neyt] Verb
To reach the highest point, summit, or highest development.

- Jenna's efforts and hard work **culminated** in her graduation.
- An amazing musical performance **culminated** the talent night.

Synonym: climax, cap, conclude, terminate, wind up
Antonym: begin, commence, open, start
Further Information
- Originated from Late Latin word *columen* meaning "top or summit."
- The synonym **climax** implies "a more intense point" than **culminate.**

cumulate: [KYOO-myuh-leyt] Verb/Adjective
To heap up or amass. (v.)
Heaped up. (adj.)

- We all need to **cumulate** the missing parts right away. (v.)
- She had the highest **cumulative** grade in the class. (adj.)

Synonym: accumulate, accrue, amass, collect, garner
Antonym: disperse, dissipate, distribute
<u>Further Information</u>
- Originated from the Latin word *cumulus* meaning "mound or heap."
- A more common form of the word is **cumulative** meaning "growing as a result of additions."

dally: [dal-ee] Verb
To waste time.
To play mockingly or playfully.

- Avoid **dallying** especially in the morning because we are always late.
- The children were told not to **dally** with the horses without any adults around.

Synonym: dawdle, delay, boondoggle, drag, idle
Antonym: complete, finish, go
<u>Further Information</u>
- Originated from the Anglo-French word *dalier* meaning "to amuse oneself."
- A related verb is **dilly-dally** which means "waste time through aimless wandering or indecision."

dearth: [durth] Noun
An inadequate supply.

- There is a **dearth** of well-trained teachers in the region.
- During hot, dry summer, there is a **dearth** of fresh produce.

Synonym: insufficiency, absence, deficiency, inadequacy, lack
Antonym: abundance, adequacy, enough, plenty, plethora
<u>Further Information</u>
- Originated from the Old English word *deore + th* meaning "precious, costly" + a suffix to indicate nouns of action, state, or quality.

REVIEW EXERCISE 10

Match the word with its synonym.

___	1.	courier	a.	vulgar
___	2.	craft	b.	crack
___	3.	craven	c.	amass
___	4.	crease	d.	expertise
___	5.	creche	e.	messenger
___	6.	credulous	f.	dawdle
___	7.	crevice	g.	naïve
___	8.	crude	h.	nursery
___	9.	culminate	i.	weak
___	10.	cumulate	j.	wrinkle
___	11.	dally	k.	climax
___	12.	dearth	l.	absence

From the words above, fill in the blanks with the most appropriate word. The word form may need changing.

1. Don is the best in the _____ of carpentry and pottery.

2. Remove the _____ on the shirt using the iron and a spray of water.

3. Many low probability events can _____ to a substantial risk.

4. The _____ was late in delivering the urgent packages.

5. The _____ knight ran away from the dragon.

6. Do not _____ in the morning or you'll miss the bus.

7. There is a _____ of crops during winter because of poor soil condition.

8. The event _____ in a beautiful performance.

9. The worm crawled into a _____ in the ground.

10. The _____ remark offended everyone

11. Little Johnny loves to go to the_____ where he gets to play with colorful toys.

12. The _____ crowd believed everything that he said.

WORD SET 11

debase: [dih-BEYS] Verb
To reduce in quality or value.
To lower in rank, dignity, or significance

- The value of the painting was **debased** because of the copycats.
- He refuses to **debase** himself by doing tasks that are beneath his rank.

Synonym: degrade, shame, cheapen, demean, demoralize
Antonym: boost, enhance, esteem, honor
Further Information
- Originated from the 1500s' word *de + base* meaning "down" + "low."
- The synonyms **demean** and **shame** imply stronger negative emotions than **debase**.

decisive: [dih-SAHY-siv] Adjective
Having the power or quality of deciding.
Characterized by or displaying no or little hesitation.

- Johnny offered a **decisive** solution to the team's urgent issues.
- The military needs men with a **decisive** manner and strong conviction.

Synonym: definite, conclusive, critical, crucial, definitive, determined, firm
Antonym: inconclusive, indefinite, ineffective
Further Information
- Evolved from the Latin word *de + caedere* meaning "off" + "to cut."
- **Decisive** should not be confused with **divisive** which means "tending to cause division or hostility between people."

decorum: [dih-KAWR-uh m] Noun
Dignified propriety of behavior, speech, dress, etc.
The quality or state of being decorous, or exhibiting such dignified propriety.

- The aristocrats are known for their **decorum** and elegant demeanor.
- The teacher was impressed with the **decorum** of the students during lunch.

Synonym: good manners, civility, correctness, decency
Antonym: immorality, impropriety, rudeness
Further Information
- Originated from the Latin word *decor* meaning "beauty, elegance or charm."
- The word **demeanor** refers to behavior and appearance in general.

deflect: [dih-FLEKT] Verb
To bend or turn aside; Turn from a straight course or straight line.

- She's very good at **deflecting** mean criticisms and ignoring rude comments.
- Neo was amazing when he **deflected** bullets in *The Matrix*.

Synonym: avert, bend, cover up, divert, pivot
Antonym: stay, straighten
Further Information
- Originated from the Latin word *de + flectere* meaning "away from" + "to bend."
- **Deflect** is related to **reflect** which means "throw back or mirror."

deliberate: [dih-LIB-er-it] Adjective/Verb
Carefully weighed or considered. (adj.)
To consider carefully. (v.)

- The **deliberate** lie is so obvious to anyone who hears it. (adj.)
- The students **deliberated** yesterday about the party theme. (v.)

Synonym: intentional, calculated, careful, cautious, conscious, meticulous
Antonym: careless, heedless, ignorant
Further Information
- Originated from the Latin word *libra* meaning "scales."
- **To deliberate** emphasizes "the use of logic and reason."

delinquent: [dih-LING-kwuh nt] Adjective/Noun
Failing in or neglectful of a duty or obligation. (adj.)
A person who is delinquent. (n.)

- The teenagers are showing **delinquent** behavior. (adj.)
- Study hard so you don't become a **delinquent** and end up being a failure. (n.)

Synonym: irresponsible, offending, overdue, tardy
Antonym: punctual
Further Information
- Originated from the Latin word *de + linquere* meaning "away" + "to leave."
- A related phrase is **juvenile delinquent** meaning "a minor who cannot be controlled by parental authority and commits antisocial or criminal acts, as vandalism or violence."

delirious: [dih-LEER-ee-uh s] Adjective
Wild with excitement, enthusiasm, etc.

- She is feeling **delirious** because of the high fever and headache.
- Maddy is **delirious** with happiness on winning the lottery.

Synonym: crazed, insane, ecstatic, thrilled, manic
Antonym: balanced, rational, reasonable, sane
Further Information
- Originated from the 1700s' word *delirium + ous* meaning "madness" + "having, full of, having to do with, doing, inclined to."
- **Delirious** implies "uncontrollable and intense emotion."

demean: [dih-MEEN] Verb
To lower in dignity, honor, or standing.

- He thinks cleaning is a **demeaning** job meant only for uneducated people.
- He **demeaned** himself by indulging in vandalism.

Synonym: humiliate, belittle, debase, degrade, despise
Antonym: uplift, improve, elevate
Further Information
- Originated from the 1600s' word *de + mean* meaning "down" + "low quality."
- **Demean** implies embarrassment or humiliation while **punishment** refers to "consequences of violation."

demeanor: [dih-MEE-ner] Noun
A conduct, behavior or attitude.

- Jimmy has a friendly **demeanor** that everybody likes and gains him many friends.
- Her **demeanor** was quite offensive to the group which caused them to boot her out.

Synonym: behavior, attitude, disposition, poise, presence
Antonym: none
Further Information
- Originated from the Old French word *de + mener* meaning "completely" + "to lead or direct."
- **Demeanor** refers to behavior or appearance in general, compared to **decorum** which means "dignified manner."

demise: [dih-MAHYZ] Noun
Termination of existence or operation; Death.

- Everybody was so surprised by her tragic **demise** during her vacation.
- The Romans brought about the **demise** of the Greeks.

Synonym: collapse, departure, dissolution, downfall, extinction, failure
Antonym: beginning, rise, start
Further Information
- Originated from the Middle French word *des + mettre* meaning "away" + "put."
- In Law, **demise** means transfer of an estate.

demote: [dih-MOHT] Verb
To reduce to a lower grade, rank, class, or position.

- One more violation and you'll be **demoted** to the lowest position.
- It is rare to **demote** an officer to a private, but it can happen.

Synonym: downgrade, bump, dismiss, relegate
Antonym: promote, keep
Further Information
- Originated in the 1880s by combining *de + promote* meaning "down" + "to advance in rank, dignity, position, etc."
- **Demote** should not be confused with **denote** which means "to signify."

denote: [dih-NOHT] Verb
To be a mark or sign of.
To be a name or designation for.

- A high fever often **denotes** viral or bacterial infection which could be serious.
- This trademark **denotes** high quality.

Synonym: designate, mean, stand for
Antonym: conceal, deny, disprove
Further Information
- Originated from the Latin word *nota* meaning "a mark."
- **Denote** should not be confused with **demote** which means "to reduce to a lower grade."

REVIEW EXERCISE 11

Match the word with its synonym.

___	1.	debase	a.	intentional
___	2.	decisive	b.	civility
___	3.	decorum	c.	downgrade
___	4.	deflect	d.	downfall
___	5.	deliberate	e.	belittle
___	6.	delinquent	f.	firm
___	7.	delirious	g.	degrade
___	8.	demean	h.	avert
___	9.	demeanor	i.	thrilled
___	10.	demise	j.	attitude
___	11.	demote	k.	offending
___	12.	denote	l.	designate

From the words above, fill in the blanks with the most appropriate word. The word form may need changing.

1. The employee was _____ because of his poor performance.

2. He felt _____ with joy after winning the competition.

3. Sam had _____ the profession by lying under oath.

4. Missy's outgoing _____ makes her the life of the party.

5. Jan refuses to be _____ from anything she had set her mind on.

6. Ancient civilizations faced _____ when attacked with military power.

7. The teenagers were charged with _____ offense because they destroyed park properties.

8. Proper _____ is necessary in classroom to ensure good learning for everyone.

9. An emergency is _____ by a loud ringing sound.

10. His _____ lie did not escape his mother.

11. He feels that war is _____ and inhumane.

12. The owner's certain and _____ actions saved the company.

WORD SET 12

depict: [dih-PIKT] Verb
To represent by or as if by painting.
To represent or characterize in words.

- The character in the novel is **depicted** as strong and independent.
- The painting **depicts** a peaceful scenery over a cliff.

Synonym: describe, render, characterize, detail, illustrate
Antonym: hide
Further Information
- Originated from the Latin word *de + pingere* meaning "completely" + "to paint."
- **Depict** may also mean "to represent something in different form."

deplete: [dih-PLEET] Verb
To decrease significantly or exhaust the abundance or supply of.

- The dry season will **deplete** the water supply soon.
- Be careful with your budget this month or it will be **depleted**.

Synonym: consumed, exhausted, drained, reduced, vacant
Antonym: energized, full
Further Information
- Originated from the Latin word *plenus* meaning "full."
- **Deplete** is commonly misspelled as **depleat** which is not a word.

deplorable: [dih-PLAWR-uh-buh l] Adjective
Causing or being a subject of grief or regret.
Causing or being a subject of censure, reproach, or disapproval.

- The news about her friend's **deplorable** accident was surprising.
- The auditorium was in a **deplorable** state after the concert.

Synonym: unfortunate, shameful, dire, disastrous, disgraceful
Antonym: acceptable, bearable, blessed
Further Information
- Originated from the Latin word *de + plorare* meaning "entirely" + "weep or cry out."
- The synonyms **unfortunate** and **shameful** imply less emotion than **deplorable**.

derivative: [dih-RIV-uh-tiv] Adjective/Noun
Not original. (adj.)
Based on another source. (n.)

- The artist's work is original and not in the slightest bit **derivative**. (adj.)
- A **derivative** is not acceptable, as we need an original solution. (n.)

Synonym: borrowed, cognate, imitative, secondary, subordinate
Antonym: important, superior
Further Information
- Originated from the Late Latin phrase *de + rivus* meaning "from" + "stream."
- In Mathematics, the **derivative** of a function represents an infinitesimal change in the function with respect to one of its variables.

derive: [dih-RAHYV] Verb
To receive or obtain from a source or origin.
To reach or obtain by reasoning.

- The wine is **derived** from a nearby winery which ensures high quality.
- The solution is **derived** from a complicated computation.

Synonym: acquire, assume, collect, determine, develop, evolve
Antonym: decrease, doubt, forfeit, give
Further Information
- Originated from the Latin word *de + rivus* meaning "from" + "stream."
- **Derive** implies "based on an original source" and is not similar to **copy**.

desist: [dih-ZIST] Verb
To stop doing something.

- The court ordered the website to **desist** from posting fake news.
- The doctors strongly encourage people to **desist** from smoking.

Synonym: stop, refrain, abstain, cease, relinquish
Antonym: carry on, complete, continue, finish
Further Information
- Originated from the Latin word *de + sistere* meaning "off" + "stop or come to a stand."
- **Desist** is typically used in Law to stop an activity.
- Usually followed by "from."

despicable: [DES-pi-kuh-buh l] Adjective
Deserving to be despised, or regarded with distaste, disgust, or disdain.

- He was a **despicable** man who treated his friends badly.
- **Despicable** actions have no place in this company.

Synonym: hateful, contemptible, degrading, disgraceful, disreputable
Antonym: good, honorable, kind, nice
<u>Further Information</u>
- Originated from the Latin word *de + spicare* meaning "down" + "to look at."
- **Despicable** implies a stronger emotion compared to **bad** or **hateful.**

destitute: [DES-ti-toot] Adjective
Without means of subsistence.
Deprived of, devoid of, or lacking.

- He overcame his **destitute** upbringing to be successful.
- The charity helps out **destitute** people in need.

Synonym: wanting, bankrupt, exhausted, impoverished
Antonym: affluent, rich
<u>Further Information</u>
- Originated from the Latin word *de + statuere* meaning "away from" + "to place."
- In scholastic works, the word **penury** is used instead of **destitution.**

deterrent: [dih-TUR-uh nt] Adjective/Noun
Serving or tending to deter. (adj.)
Military strength or an ability to defend a country or retaliate strongly enough to prevent an enemy from attacking. (n.)

- Is a security system an effective **deterrent** against home invasion? (adj.)
- The government set up a **deterrent** against terrorists. (n.)

Synonym: impediment, disincentive, hindrance, obstacle
Antonym: assistance, help
<u>Further Information</u>
- Originated from the Latin word *de + terrere* meaning "away" + "frighten."
- **Deterrent** implies "something that keeps something away" compared to **obstacle** which means "something that hinders progress."

detrimental: [de-truh-MEN-tl] Adjective/Noun
Causing loss or injury. (adj.)
A detrimental person or thing. (n.)

- The **detrimental** decision made her lose the case.
- Miscommunication is **detrimental** to their relationship.

Synonym: damaging, adverse, destructive, disturbing
Antonym: aiding, assisting, favorable, friendly
Further Information
- Originated from the Latin word *de + terrere* meaning "away" + "to rub or wear."
- **Detrimental** is commonly misspelled as **determental** which is not a word.

deviate: [DEE-vee-eyt] Verb/Adjective/Noun
To turn aside, as from a route, way, course, etc. (v.)
Characterized by deviation or departure from an accepted norm or standard, as of behavior. (adj.)
A person or thing that departs from the accepted norm or standard. (n.)

- If we **deviate** from the suggestions in the map, we will get lost. (v.)
- A **deviated** septum is a serious medical condition affecting millions. (adj.)
- They thought he's a **deviate** just because he lives in the woods far from people. (n.)

Synonym: depart, differ, diverge, vary, veer
Antonym: agree, stay
Further Information
- Originated from the Late Latin word *de + via* meaning "away from" + "way."
- Should not be confused with **devious** meaning "dishonest."

devious: [DEE-vee-uh s] Adjective
(Of route or journey) Departing from the most direct way.
Showing a skillful use of underhand tactics to achieve goals.

- Jamie figured that he needs to be **devious** to win the competition.
- There is a **devious** plot to overthrow the government and create unrest.

Synonym: dishonest, calculating, deceitful, fraudulent, insidious, indirect
Antonym: fair, forthright, frank, honest, direct
Further Information
- Originated from the Latin word *de + via* meaning "away from" + "way."
- Should not be confused with **dubious** which means "hesitating or doubting."

REVIEW EXERCISE 12

Match the word with its synonym.

___	1. depict	a.	impoverished
___	2. depleted	b.	hateful
___	3. deplorable	c.	deceitful
___	4. derivative	d.	exhausted
___	5. derive	e.	shameful
___	6. desist	f.	adverse
___	7. despicable	g.	hindrance
___	8. destitute	h.	obtain
___	9. deterrent	i.	imitative
___	10. detrimental	j.	depart
___	11. deviate	k.	describe
___	12. devious	l.	cease

From the words above, fill in the blanks with the most appropriate word. The word form may need changing.

1. Water supplies are typically _____ during hot summers.

2. After losing all his money and assets, he is now considered a _____.

3. His research is a _____ of another project.

4. The scientists tried to _____ the medicine from the leaves of wild herbs.

5. The _____ bully was disliked by all students.

6. Victor is known as cunning and _____ businessman.

7. Eating too much sugar can be _____ to your health.

8. Some plants are known natural pest _____.

9. Stealing is a _____ act that will surely put you in jail.

10. If you want to lose weight, you should _____ from eating junk food.

11. He _____ from the suggestion and followed his own instincts.

12. The photograph _____ a beautiful countryside scene.

WORD SET 13

devoid: [dih-VOID] Adjective/Verb
Not possessing, untouched by, void, or destitute. (adj.)
Entirely lacking or free from. (v.)

- The desert is currently **devoid** of plant life. (adj.)
- He kept his voice **devoid** of emotion. (v.)

Synonym: empty, wanting, bare, barren, lacking
Antonym: full
Further Information
- Originated from the Old French word *des + voider* meaning "out or way" + "to empty."
- It is commonly used in the phrasal verb **devoid of.**

devout: [dih-VOUT] Adjective
Devoted to divine worship or service.
Earnest or sincere.

- My family is **devout** Catholic and we go to Church every Sunday.
- He expressed his **devout** allegiance to the political party.

Synonym: adoring, ardent, faithful, fervent, passionate, pious
Antonym: apathetic, cold, cool, dishonest, disloyal
Further Information
- Originated from the Old French word *de + vovere* meaning "down, away" + "to vow."
- Should not be confused with **devote** which means "give all or a large part of one's time or resources to."

dialect: [DAHY-uh-lekt] Noun
A variety of a language that is distinguished from other varieties of the same language by features of phonology, grammar, vocabulary and usage.

- It is quite challenging to understand his **dialect**.
- Some **dialects** sound similar and have the same grammar rules.

Synonym: accent, idiom, jargon, local language, lingo, speech
Antonym: standard
Further Information
- Originated from the Latin *dia + legein* meaning "across or between" + "speak."
- **Dialect** is "a regional variety of a language" while a **language** is "a distinct body of words and system of communication."

dichotomy: [dahy-KOT-uh-mee] Noun
Division into two parts, kinds, etc.
Division into two mutually exclusive, opposed, or contradictory groups.

- You have to remember that there is a **dichotomy** between intent and action.
- The homework should discuss the **dichotomy** of social theory and practice.

Synonym: division
Antonym: agreement
Further Information
- Originated from the Greek word *dicha+ temnein* meaning "in two, apart" + "to cut."
- In Botany, **dichotomy** is "a mode of branching as in plants or stems."

dilate: [dahy-LEYT] Verb
To make wider or larger.
To spread out.

- When Jimmy is shocked, his eyes become big and **dilated**.
- The pipes need to be replaced because they are **dilating**.

Synonym: stretch, widen, expand, swell
Antonym: abbreviate, abridge, compress
Further Information
- Originated from the Latin word *di + latus* meaning "apart" + "wide."
- **Dilate** implies "widening or stretching something that is narrow."

diligent: [DIL-i-juh nt] Adjective
Constant in effort to accomplish something.
Done or pursued with persevering attention.

- **Diligent** students typically succeed in life and enjoy amazing careers.
- The painting shows the artist's **diligent** efforts and creativity.

Synonym: active, hardworking, assiduous, attentive, painstaking
Antonym: careless, disinterested, idle, ignorant
Further Information
- Originated from the Latin word *dis + legere* meaning "apart" + "choose or gather."
- **Diligent** implies "hard and careful work "done with or employing great care and thoroughness."

diminutive: [dih-MIN-yuh-tiv] Adjective/Noun
To be small or tiny. (adj.)
A small thing or a short person. (n.)

- With all the tall structures, the nearby house looks **diminutive**. (adj.)
- The name *Will* is a **diminutive** of *William*. (n.)

Synonym: tiny, petite, miniature, pint-sized
Antonym: big, enormous, giant
Further Information
- Evolved from the Latin word *de + minuere* meaning "completely" + "make small."
- In Grammar, **diminutive** pertains to a form denoting smallness like the suffix *-let*. (As in *drop-let* from *drop*.)

dingy: [DIN-jee] Adjective
Of a dark, dull, or dirty color or aspect.

- This apartment is quite **dingy**; let's look for another one.
- You need to wash that cap because it looks **dingy**.

Synonym: soiled, tacky, dilapidated, dirty, drab
Antonym: bright, clean, good, nice
Further Information
- Originated from the Old English word *dynge* meaning "dung."
- Should not be confused with **dinghy** which is "a type of small boat."

diplomatic: [dip-luh-MAT-ik] Adjective
Of, relating to, or engaged in diplomacy.
Skilled in dealing with sensitive matters or people.

- He's elected as a leader because he's **diplomatic**.
- The **diplomatic** relationship between countries is very important.

Synonym: politic, tactful, conciliatory, gracious, polite
Antonym: rude
Further Information
- Originated from the Greek word *diploos + -oma* meaning "double" + a suffix forming neuter nouns.
- A person who deals with the relationship between two or more groups is called a **diplomat.**

disadvantaged: [dis-uh d-VAN-tijd] Adjective/Noun
Lacking the normal or usual necessities and comforts of life, such as proper housing, educational opportunities, job security, adequate medical care, etc. (adj.)
Disadvantaged persons collectively. (n.)

- His **disadvantaged** lifestyle is not an obstacle to his goals. (adj.)
- The soup kitchen is not open to accept the **disadvantaged**. (n.)

Synonym: underprivileged, deprived, handicapped
Antonym: rich, strong
Further Information
- Originated from the Old French word *des + avantage* meaning "lack of" + "position of being in advance of another."
- **Disadvantaged** is a more polite synonym of the words **poor** or **destitute**.

discard: [dih-SKAHRD] Verb/Noun
To cast aside or dispose of. (v.)
A person or thing that is cast out or rejected. (n.)

- You need to **discard** fruits that are not up to standards. (v.)
- The traitor was banished from the kingdom to live with other **discards** in the forest. (n.)

Synonym: abandon, cancel, dispose, ditch, dump
Antonym: accept, allow, approve, choose
Further Information
- Originated from the English word *dis + card* meaning "away" + "playing card."
- Should not be confused with **discord** which means "disagreement between people."

disdain: [dis-DEYN] Verb/Noun
To look upon or treat with contempt. (v.)
A feeling of contempt for anything regarded as unworthy. (n.)

- She **disdains** mass produced products and opts for organic ones. (v.)
- He expressed **disdain** towards his brother because of their argument. (n.)

Synonym: hate, indifference, antipathy, arrogance, aversion
Antonym: admiration, affection, approval, flattery
Further Information
- Originated from the Old French word *des + deignier* meaning "do the opposite" + "treat as worthy."
- **Disdain** is an expression of both indifference and hate.

REVIEW EXERCISE 13

Match the word with its synonym.

___	1.	devoid	a.	abandon
___	2.	devout	b.	hate
___	3.	dialect	c.	faithful
___	4.	dichotomy	d.	widen
___	5.	dilate	e.	tiny
___	6.	diligent	f.	dirty
___	7.	diminutive	g.	division
___	8.	dingy	h.	deprived
___	9.	diplomatic	i.	empty
___	10.	disadvantaged	j.	politic
___	11.	discard	k.	speech
___	12.	disdain	l.	attentive

From the words above, fill in the blanks with the most appropriate word. The word form may need changing.

1. He is a _____ believer in hard-work and perseverance.

2. George is a _____ student that's why he always receives good grade.

3. There are several _____ of Chinese some of which are mutually unintelligible.

4. Countries always try to maintain _____ relationships with each other.

5. The couple bought a huge house that made their apartment seem _____.

6. Lea felt _____ towards the unfair treatment of the citizens.

7. I_____ my old suit and bought a new one.

8. The forest is _____ of any humans but teeming with animals.

9. A lot of poor students are _____ in developing their abilities fully.

10. A person's eyes _____ when he is excited.

11. The crew is cleaning up the _____ building.

12. There is a clear _____ between what's right and what's wrong.

WORD SET 14

disembark: [dis-em-BAHRK] Verb
To go ashore from a ship.
To remove or unload (cargo or passengers) from a ship, aircraft, or other vehicle.

- We **disembarked** on a beautiful beach with coconut trees lining the whole area.
- The captain announced that the passengers should **disembark** due to an emergency.

Synonym: alight, dismount, get off
Antonym: embark, get on
Further Information
- Originated from the Latin word *des + barca* meaning "to do the opposite" + "ship's boat."
- **Disembark** is typically used when getting off a boat or a ship.

disinclination: [dis-in-kluh-NEY-shuh n] Noun
The lack of enthusiasm.

- He felt a strong **disinclination** to further his studies and chose to start working full time right away.
- She showed a **disinclination** to face up to her issues.

Synonym: unwillingness, alienation, antipathy, aversion, demur
Antonym: approval, happiness, inclination
Further Information
- Negative form of the 1300s' word *in + clinare* meaning "into" + "to bend."
- **Disinclination** is similar to **disinterest**.

disingenuous: [dis-in-JEN-yoo-uh s] Adjective
Lacking in frankness, candor, or sincerity.

- Tom's excuse is rather **disingenuous** and unsupported by facts.
- The student's **disingenuous** reason for missing the deadline was not believed by the teacher.

Synonym: insincere, deceitful, dishonest, false, unfair
Antonym: fair, frank, honest, ingenuous
Further Information
- Originated from the 1600s' word *dis + ingenuus* meaning "opposite" + "noble in nature, high-minded."
- An informal synonym of **disingenuous** is **fake.**

disown: [dis-OHN] Verb
To refuse to acknowledge as belonging or pertaining to oneself.

- The family **disowned** him because of his crimes.
- He **disowned** his previous statement and told the truth.

Synonym: disavow, discard, disclaim, renounce, repudiate, reject
Antonym: admit, allow, approve
Further Information
- Originated from the Old English word *dis + agen* meaning "lack of" + "one's own."
- **Reject** is an informal synonym of **disown.**

disparage: [dih-SPAR-ij] Verb
To speak of or treat badly.
To bring reproach or discredit upon.

- It's mean to **disparage** one's achievements and belittle their efforts.
- Do not **disparage** anyone's efforts as it can burn bridges.

Synonym: belittle, criticize, decry, defame, degrade
Antonym: admire, approve, commend
Further Information
- Negative form of the Latin word *par* meaning "equal."
- **Disparage** is a special type of **insult** that shows the insulter as superior.

dissect: [dih-SEKT] Verb
To cut apart (an animal body, plant, etc.) in order to examine the structure, relation of parts etc.
To analyze in minute detail.

- Before applying their proposed solution, we need to **dissect** each part.
- She hated **dissecting** the samples in her biology class.

Synonym: cut up, anatomize, cut, disjoin, dismember
Antonym: combine, connect
Further Information
- Originated from the Latin word *dis + secare* meaning "apart" + "to cut."
- **Dissect** is to "cut up something that is whole into parts" while **separate** is "to create distance from one to another."

distinguished: [dih-STING-gwisht] Adjective
Made conspicuous by excellence.
Having an air of dignity or eminence.

- Please welcome our **distinguished** alumni and celebrated faculty.
- He is a **distinguished** member of the community who is liked by everyone.

Synonym: famous, outstanding, acclaimed, brilliant, dignified
Antonym: infamous, insignificant, lowly
Further Information
- Originated from the Latin word *dis + stinguere* meaning "apart" + "put out."
- **Distinguished** implies "fame or being unique because of excellence or achievement."

divinity: [dih-VIN-i-tee] Noun
The quality of being holy.
Religious studies.

- They persuaded him to study mathematics instead of **divinity**.
- Most religions center on worshipping **divinity**.

Synonym: absolute, deity, sanctity, godliness
Antonym: devil, evil
Further Information
- Originated from the Latin word *divinus* meaning "belonging to a deity."
- Its root word **divine** implies holiness and goodness.

divulge: [dih-VUHLJ] Verb
To disclose or reveal.

- The accused is required by the court to **divulge** all information about the case.
- She was surprised by the secrets **divulged** by her friend.

Synonym: admit, confess, disclose, leak, blab
Antonym: conceal, cover, hide, keep
Further Information
- Originated from the Latin word *dis + vulgare* meaning "apart" + + "make common property."
- **Divulge** implies revelation of something that is previously unknown or secret.

dogmatic: [dawg-MAT-ik] Adjective
Relating to any strong set of principles concerning faith, morals, etc.
Asserting opinions in a rigid or arrogant manner.

- It is common to hear **dogmatic** arguments from opposite political parties.
- I refuse to argue with someone who is so **dogmatic**.

Synonym: dictatorial, arbitrary, arrogant, assertive, categorical
Antonym: ambiguous, equivocal, impartial
Further Information
- Originated from the Greek word *dokein* meaning "to seem good or think."
- Being **dogmatic** stems from the belief that one's opinion is absolute and accurate.

doleful: [DOHL-fuh l] Adjective
Something that is sorrowful or mournful.

- Why does she have a **doleful** look on her face?
- The failure of the project put him in a **doleful** mood.

Synonym: depressing, afflicted, cheerless, crestfallen
Antonym: cheerful, elated
Further Information
- Originated from the Latin word *dolere* meaning "suffer or grieve."
- The synonym **depressing** implies a more negative emotion.

domestic: [duh-MES-tik] Adjective/Noun
Of or relating to the home, the household, household affairs, or the family; Something produced or manufactured in one's own country. (adj.)
A person paid to help with cleaning and other household chores. (n.)

- Playing board games with the family is such a **domestic** pleasure. (adj.)
- All the cleaning was undertaken by the **domestic.** (n.)

Synonym: household, private, home, local
Antonym: none
Further Information
- Originated from the Latin word *domus* meaning "house."
- **Domestic** can also be used to refer to something that is within a territory or a country.

REVIEW EXERCISE 14

Match the word with its synonym.

___	1.	disembark	a.	belittle
___	2.	disinclination	b.	unwillingness
___	3.	disingenuous	c.	deceitful
___	4.	disown	d.	local
___	5.	disparage	e.	godliness
___	6.	dissect	f.	dismount
___	7.	distinguished	g.	reject
___	8.	divinity	h.	dictatorial
___	9.	divulge	i.	cheerless
___	10.	dogmatic	j.	disclose
___	11.	doleful	k.	famous
___	12.	domestic	l.	disjoin

From the words above, fill in the blanks with the most appropriate word. The word form may need changing.

1. His parents _____ him because of his criminal behavior.

2. Sarah did not really enjoy _____ frogs in laboratory.

3. Some excuses are obviously _____ and can be caught out easily.

4. All passengers had to _____ from the ship due to a technical problem.

5. She had a _____ for sports but loved music.

6. _____ flights are definitely a lot cheaper than international flights.

7. "A top secret should never be _____ to anyone at any cost," said the spy.

8. His assertions were too _____ and inflexible.

9. Most religious orders revolve around a _____.

10. Professor Lee is a _____ member of the university.

11. He was _____ the whole day because his pet goldfish died.

12. It is not kind to _____ anyone in public.

WORD SET 15

drab: [drab] Adjective/Noun
To be dull or cheerless. (v.)
Any of several fabrics of light greyish-brown color, especially of thick wool or cotton. (n.)

- Why do you always wear that **drab** grey shirt that looks so boring? (v.)
- A young man dressed in **drabs**. (n.)

Synonym: dull, colorless, bleak, desolate, dingy
Antonym: bright, cheerful, clean
Further Information
- Originated from the Old French word *drap* meaning "cloth."
- **Drab** is similar to **boring.**

draft: [draft] Noun/Verb
The initial or preliminary version of a drawing, document or design. (n.)
To create the initial version of a drawing, document or design. (v.)

- My first **draft** of the essay was very basic and more work was required. (n.)
- **Draft** your ideas and submit them by tomorrow afternoon. (v.)

Synonym: blueprint, plant, outline, version
Antonym: none
Further Information
- Originated from the Old Norse word *drattr* meaning "to draw."
- **Draft** may be confused with **Draught** which sounds the same but means "a current of air."

drench: [drench] Verb/Noun
To wet thoroughly. (v.)
A dose of medicine administered to an animal. (n.)

- The rain was so sudden that we were **drenched**. (v.)
- The veterinarian administered a worming **drench** to the cows. (n.)

Synonym: deluge, douse, drown, immerse
Antonym: dehydrate, dry
Further Information
- Originated from the Germanic word *drenc* meaning "drink or draft."
- **Drench** means to "make very wet" whereas **flood** means "a (usually disastrous) overflow of water."

dwindle: [DWIN-dl] Verb
To become smaller and smaller.

- I didn't notice that the candies in the jar **dwindled** to almost nothing.
- Due to excessive rainfall and flooding, the crops **dwindled** and failed.

Synonym: waste away, abate, decay, decline, decrease
Antonym: ascend, develop, enhance
Further Information
- Originated from the Middle English *dwinen* meaning "waste away or fade."
- Should not be confused with **dindle** which means "to tingle or vibrate, such as a loud sound does."

earnest: [UR-nist] Adjective/Noun
Serious in intention, purpose, or effort. (adj.)
Full seriousness, as of intention or purpose. (n.)

- John is known to be an **earnest** worker and an honest person. (adj.)
- You need to speak in **earnest** to be taken seriously. (n.)

Synonym: ardent, diligent, fervent, heartfelt
Antonym: apathetic, cold, cool
Further Information
- Originated from the Old Norse *ern* meaning "able or vigorous."
- **Earnest** is commonly misspelled as **ernest** which is a male name.

ebb: [eb] Noun/Verb
A flowing backward or away. (n.)
To flow back or away, as the water of a tide. (v.)

- The **ebb** of the once great culture can be seen in the old dilapidated structures. (n.)
- The water is **ebbing** towards the sea in a slow, hypnotic manner. (v.)

Synonym: regression, decline, abatement, backflow, decay, recede
Antonym: advance, development, enlargement
Further Information
- Originated from the Old English *ebba* meaning "falling of the tide."
- **Ebb and flow** are "two phases of the tide or any similar movement of water."

economy: [ih-KON-uh-mee] Noun/Adjective
Frugality in the expenditure or consumption of money, materials, etc.; Management of the resources of a community, country, etc. (n.)
Costing less to make, buy, or operate. (adj.)

- He attempted to combine good living with **economy**. (n.)
- Could I book an **economy** car for the trip? (adj.)

Synonym: saving, frugality, recession, industry, wealth
Antonym: addition, carelessness, disregard
Further Information
- Originated from the Greek words *oikos* and *nemein* meaning "house" and "manage."
- **Economy** may also refer to "the management of financial and other resources of a group or area."

eerie: [EER-ee] Adjective
Uncanny, so as to inspire superstitious fear.

- I'm not happy that we are in an **eerie** forest at night.
- Hearing a midnight owl hoot is quite **eerie** and creepy.

Synonym: spooky, bizarre, creepy, fantastic, ghostly
Antonym: common, earthly, familiar
Further Information
- Originated from the Old Frisian word *erg* meaning "evil or bad."
- Can also be spelled as **eery**.

effervescent: [ef-er-VES-uh nt] Adjective
(Of a liquid) Giving off bubbles of gas.

- This mineral water is quite **effervescent** and gives off a strong smell.
- The perfume that you just bought is very **effervescent**.

Synonym: fizzing, foaming, airy, bouncy, bubbly
Antonym: flat
Further Information
- Originated from the Latin word *ex + fervescere* meaning "out" + "begin to boil."
- An **effervescent** personality means someone who is lively and enthusiastic.

elegant: [EL-i-guh nt] Adjective
Tastefully fine or luxurious in dress, style, design, etc.
Gracefully refined and dignified, as in tastes, habits, or literary style.

- An **elegant** young gentleman just arrived, greeting everyone in the party.
- The design of the building is quite **elegant** and sophisticated.

Synonym: chic, beautiful, classic, dignified, exquisite
Antonym: common, dull, inferior
Further Information
- Originated from the Latin *elegans* meaning "dainty, fastidious."
- **Elegant** may refer to behavior, taste, or style.

eloquence: [EL-uh-kwuh ns] Noun
The practice or art of using language with fluency and aptness.

- The candidate showed his **eloquence** during the elections.
- A certain level of **eloquence** takes time and effort to perfect.

Synonym: expressiveness, fervor, fluency, passion, poise
Antonym: none
Further Information
- Originated from the Latin word *ex + loqui* meaning "out" + "to speak."
- **Eloquence** often refers to the ability to speak well in public.

embargo: [em-BAHR-goh] Noun/Verb
An order of a government prohibiting trade or other commercial activity. (n.)
To impose an embargo on. (v.)

- There was an announcement of **embargo** due to the storm. (n.)
- Due to the sudden announcement, many ships were **embargoed**. (v.)

Synonym: ban, restraint
Antonym: aid
Further Information
- Originated from *in + barra* meaning "within" + "a bar."
- **Embargo** is only used for commercial activity whereas **ban** is a general term for restriction.

REVIEW EXERCISE 15

Match the word with its synonym.

___	1. drab	a.	recede
___	2. draft	b.	ban
___	3. drench	c.	douse
___	4. dwindle	d.	outline
___	5. earnest	e.	exquisite
___	6. ebb	f.	bubbly
___	7. economy	g.	decline
___	8. eerie	h.	fluency
___	9. effervescent	i.	spooky
___	10. elegant	j.	wealth
___	11. eloquence	k.	colorless
___	12. embargo	l.	diligent

From the words above, fill in the blanks with the most appropriate word. The word form may need changing.

1. His graduation speech showed his _____ and was greeted with a standing ovation.

2. The _____ of the family's new house was created by a popular architect.

3. He studied in _____ and passed with flying colors.

4. Mary has an _____ and outgoing personality.

5. Water level in the lake will _____ during the dry season.

6. Her gray dress is quite _____ for her flashy taste.

7. I was _____ during the storm.

8. The number of birds in the city _____ as the number of people increased.

9. Ships were stranded because of the _____.

10. The _____ of the town is booming this year, due to increased tourism.

11. The old house is quite _____ at night.

12. Queens are normally thought to be _____ and stylish.

WORD SET 16

embellish: [em-BEL-ish] Verb
To beautify by adding decorative details or features.

- The cake is **embellished** with colorful candies and tasty marshmallows.
- Do not **embellish** your speech too much, as it can get boring.

Synonym: adorn, bedeck, embroider, overstate
Antonym: decrease, harm, lessen, reduce
Further Information
- Originated from the Latin *bellus* meaning "handsome or pretty."
- In literature, **embellish** means "to enhance by adding fine details."

embezzle: [em-BEZ-uh l] Verb
To appropriate fraudulently to one's own use, such as money or property entrusted to one's care.

- They found out about the plan to **embezzle** the company funds.
- The thieves **embezzled** a large amount of money.

Synonym: steal, filch, appropriate, loot, pilfer
Antonym: give, receive
Further Information
- Originated from the Old French word *em + besillier* meaning "into" + "torment or destroy."
- **Embezzlement** is a type of stealing by misappropriating or misusing money.

empathetic: [em-puh-THET-ik] Adjective
Identification with the feelings, thoughts, or attitudes of others.

- Mary is **empathetic** to the situation of the victims of the disaster.
- The children like talking to the **empathetic** counselor.

Synonym: understanding, compassionate, sensitive
Antonym: indifferent, merciless

Further Information
- Originated from the Greek word *in + pathos* meaning "in" + "feeling."
- **Empathetic** is similar but not identical to **sympathetic.**
  Empathetic means "putting yourself in the shoes of another" whereas **sympathetic** means "feeling sorrow for hardships of another."

encrypt: [en-KRIPT] Verb
To encipher or encode.

- Make sure that your files are **encrypted** before transferring them.
- This software will **encrypt** your messages before sending them.

Synonym: encode, encipher
Antonym: decipher, decode
Further Information
- Originated from the Greek word *en + kruptos* meaning "in" + "hidden."
- **Encryption** involves creating a hidden message or information.

endorse: [en-DAWRS] Verb
To approve, support, or sustain.

- This bakery must be good for it to be **endorsed** by a celebrity.
- The report was **endorsed** by the college.

Synonym: support, authorize, advocate, affirm, approve
Antonym: attack, censure, criticize, deny
Further Information
- Originated from the Latin word *in + dorsum* meaning "in or on" + "back."
- In Law, endorse means "to sign one's name on (a commercial document or other instrument)."
- It may also be spelled as **indorse.**

enduring: [en-DOOR-ing] Adjective
To be lasting or permanent.

- His work has an **enduring** effect on people which makes him memorable.
- The successful businessman formed **enduring** relationships with his customers.

Synonym: lasting, abiding, permanent
Antonym: temporary
Further Information
- Originated from the Latin *in + durus* meaning "in" + "hard."
- **Enduring** may also mean "suffer patiently."

engender: [en-JEN-der] Verb
To produce, cause, or give rise to.

- A heart full of hate **engenders** prejudice and inspires violence.
- The restaurant is giving away free dessert to **engender** interest from potential customers.

Synonym: cause, arouse, beget, breed, foment
Antonym: calm, destroy, discourage
Further Information
- Originated from the Latin word *in + generare* meaning "in" + "generate."
- Should not be confused with **endanger** meaning "to expose to danger."

engulfed: [en-GUHLF] Verb
To swallow up; To surround completely.
To plunge or immerse.

- The disastrous tsunami **engulfed** many villages and towns in its path.
- There's an upcoming test, so he **engulfed** himself in studies.

Synonym: absorb, overwhelm, bury, consume, encompass
Antonym: dry, neglect
Further Information
- Originated from the 1500s' word *en + gulf* meaning "put in" + "gulf."
- **Engulfed** has similar meaning to the phrasal verbs **swallow up**, **soak up**, and **suck in**.

enmity: [EN-mi-tee] Noun
A feeling or condition of hostility.

- The competing teams showed **enmity** towards one another.
- **Enmity** is easily solved by open communication and compromise.

Synonym: hatred, animosity, acrimony, alienation, animus
Antonym: approval, friendliness, friendship
Further Information
- Originated from the Old French word *enemite* meaning "hostile feeling."
- The exact opposite of **enmity** is **amity** meaning "friendship."

ensuing: [en-SOO-ing] Adjective
An event or activity that happens after something else, often as a result of it.

- They tried a risky solution which was the cause of the **ensuing** problems the next day.
- The storm was terrifying, and the **ensuing** wreckage took months to clear.

Synonym: resultant, coming, consequent, subsequent
Antonym: antecedent, preceding
Further Information
- Originated from the Latin word *sequi* meaning "follow."
- **Ensuing** is a result of a previous event while **following** is a general term for "what comes next."

enthralling: [en-THRAWL-ing] Adjective
Holding one's attention completely.

- The **enthralling** performance earned a standing ovation.
- She was quite an **enthralling** conversationalist.

Synonym: absorbing, captivating, engrossing, fascinating, gripping
Antonym: boring, repulsive, uninteresting
Further Information
- Originated from Old English *en + thrall* meaning "to put in" + "a person who is in bondage."
- **Enthralling** implies "something interesting enough to hold one's complete attention" while **thrilling** means "causing feeling of sudden excitement."

enthusiastic: [en-thoo-zee-AS-tik] Adjective
Full of or characterized by interest or excitement.

- He is very **enthusiastic** about his new job.
- An **enthusiastic** child showed interest in participating in class.

Synonym: interested, excited, ardent, avid, eager
Antonym: apathetic, cold, cool, disinterested, dispassionate
Further Information
- Originated from the Greek word *enthous* meaning "possessed by a god."
- An older usage means "to a person possessed by a god, or someone who exhibited intense piety."

REVIEW EXERCISE 16

Match the word with its synonym.

___	1.	embellish	a.	absorb
___	2.	embezzle	b.	lasting
___	3.	empathetic	c.	excited
___	4.	encrypt	d.	encode
___	5.	endorse	e.	advocate
___	6.	enduring	f.	absorbing
___	7.	engender	g.	steal
___	8.	engulfed	h.	adorn
___	9.	enmity	i.	animosity
___	10.	ensuing	j.	arouse
___	11.	enthralling	k.	compassionate
___	12.	enthusiastic	l.	consequent

From the words above, fill in the blanks with the most appropriate word. The word form may need changing.

1. The vice president is guilty of _____ money from the company.

2. Celebrities often _____ products that they love and regularly use.

3. The town is _____ in a thick blanket of fog.

4. Everyone is _____ to his loss and tragedy.

5. Some inventors and scientists have an _____ effect on the world.

6. The _____ between the two groups was resolved by compromise.

7. It was _____ to see the circus performance and stunts.

8. Interests and hobbies of earlier years _____ successful careers later on.

9. He _____ the Christmas tree with cute baubles.

10. It is necessary to _____ secret messages.

11. I am happy to see that you are _____ about joining the team.

12. After the accident, the _____ investigation was gruelling and complicated.

WORD SET 17

enumerate: [ih-NOO-muh-reyt] Verb
To mention separately, as in counting.

- Can you **enumerate** the supplies that we will need for the trip?
- The teacher **enumerated** four objectives for the year.

Synonym: list, count, calculate, itemize, recite
Antonym: conceal, estimate, guess
Further Information
- Originated from the Latin word *ex + numerus* meaning "out" + "number."
- Should not be confused with **remunerate** meaning "to pay, recompense, or reward for work, trouble, etc."

epoch: [EP-uhk] Noun
A particular period of time marked by distinctive features, events, etc.

- The popularity of streaming websites and applications marks the end of the **epoch** of the DVD format.
- The Renaissance is an **epoch** of innovation and transformation.

Synonym: period, age, era, span, time
Antonym: none
Further Information
- Originated from the Greek word *epi + ekhein* meaning "on" + "to hold."
- Should not be confused with **epic** meaning "noting or pertaining to a long poetic composition."

equine: [EE-kwahyn] Adjective/Noun
Of, relating to, or resembling a horse. (adj.)
A horse. (n.)

- There is an ongoing **equine** flu outbreak in the county during the winter. (adj.)
- That is a beautiful **equine** in your farm. Is it for sale? (n.)

Synonym: horse, roan
Antonym: none

Further Information
- Originated from the Latin word *equus* meaning "horse."
- **Equine** is for horses, as **feline** is for cats and **canine** is for dogs.

equivocal: [ih-KWIV-uh-kuh l] Adjective
Allowing the possibility of several different meanings, as a word or phrase.

- The **equivocal** statements of politicians often confuse the public.
- The instruction was too **equivocal**; that's why I failed to solve the problem.

Synonym: doubtful, uncertain, ambiguous, ambivalent, dubious
Antonym: certain, clear, definite
Further Information
- Originated from the Latin word *aequus + vocare* meaning "equally" + "to call."
- The exact opposite of **equivocal** is **unequivocal** meaning "absolute or clear."

err: [ur]/[er] Verb
To go astray in thought or belief.
To make a mistake.

- To **err** is human; to forgive, divine.
- I accidentally **erred** when calculating my tax and had to redo everything.

Synonym: misbehave, miscalculate, stray, stumble
Antonym: behave, obey, stay
Further Information
- Originated from the Latin word *errare* meaning "to stray."
- Should not be confused with **error** which means "deviation from accuracy or correctness."

errand: [ER-uh nd] Noun
A short and quick trip to accomplish a specific purpose.

- I'm swamped with **errands** today; I can't rest.
- I reduce my **errands** on weekends by going to the grocery store after work.

Synonym: task, assignment, charge, commission, duty
Antonym: none
Further Information
- Originated from the Old English word *ærende* meaning "message or mission."
- **Errand** implies "short and easy task."

erratic: [ih-RAT-ik] Adjective
Deviating from the usual or proper course in conduct or opinion.

- She was showing **erratic** behavior during her shift at work.
- Observe if a car is driving in an **erratic** manner and report to me immediately.

Synonym: unpredictable, wandering, abnormal, arbitrary, bizarre
Antonym: calm, common, normal
Further Information
- Originated from the Latin word *errare* meaning "to stray or err."
- **Erratic** implies "inconsistent and unpredictable."

ethnic: [ETH-nik] Adjective
Pertaining to or characteristic of a people, especially a group.

- Pupils from a wide variety of **ethnic** backgrounds study in the school.
- The **ethnic** minority is requesting protection from people encroaching upon their lands.

Synonym: racial, indigenous, tribal, native
Antonym: none
Further Information
- Originated from the Greek word *ethnos* meaning "nation."
- The related word **indigenous** means "born or native to a land or region" while **ethnic** means "relating to a group."

evince: [ih-VINS] Verb
To show clearly; make evident or manifest.

- His letters **evince** the excitement he felt at winning the trophy.
- It was exciting to see children **evince** an interest in science.

Synonym: manifest, attest, declare, demonstrate
Antonym: conceal, cover, deny
Further Information
- Originated from the Latin word *ex + vincere* meaning "out" + "to overcome."
- The adjective form **evincible** which means "to show clearly" should not be confused with **invincible** which means "something which cannot be defeated."

exacerbate: [ig-ZAS-er-beyt] Verb
To increase the severity, bitterness, or violence of.

- Touching a burned skin will **exacerbate** the pain and infection.
- The statement given by the president will **exacerbate** the tense relationship with other countries.

Synonym: infuriate, aggravate, annoy, heighten, inflame
Antonym: aid, alleviate, appease
<u>Further Information</u>
- Originated from the Latin word *ex + acerbus* meaning "out" + "harsh or bitter."
- In Medicine, exacerbation means "the worsening of a disease or an increase in its symptoms."

excavate: [EKS-kuh-veyt] Verb
To make hollow by removing the inner part.
To dig or scoop out (earth, sand, etc.)

- They are planning to **excavate** a site where ancient potteries were found.
- The city government requires a permit if you want to **excavate** near a busy street.

Synonym: scrape, shovel, uncover, unearth, dig up
Antonym: cover, fill
<u>Further Information</u>
- Originated from the Latin word *cavus* meaning "hollow."
- In archaeology, **excavation**, which is the noun form of **excavate**, is the exposure, processing and recording of archaeological remains.

exonerate: [ig-ZON-uh-reyt] Verb
To clear, as of an accusation.
To relieve, as from an obligation, duty, or task.

- The judge is about to **exonerate** an innocent man.
- He's waiting for his manager to **exonerate** him from his duties so he can go home early.

Synonym: excuse, absolve, acquit, dismiss, discharge
Antonym: blame, condemn, convict
<u>Further Information</u>
- Originated from the Latin word *ex + onus* meaning "from" + "a burden."
- **Exonerate** is typically used in proceedings with the law.

REVIEW EXERCISE 17

Match the word with its synonym.

___	1.	enumerate	a.	uncertain
___	2.	epoch	b.	manifest
___	3.	equine	c.	horse
___	4.	equivocal	d.	racial
___	5.	err	e.	task
___	6.	errand	f.	aggravate
___	7.	erratic	g.	unpredictable
___	8.	ethnic	h.	uncover
___	9.	evince	i.	miscalculate
___	10.	exacerbate	j.	list
___	11.	excavate	k.	age
___	12.	exonerate	l.	absolve

From the words above, fill in the blanks with the most appropriate word. The word form may need changing.

1. The horse farm is looking to hire a vet with experience in _____ care.

2. His _____ behavior is concerning and should be monitored.

3. When driving in snow, it is better to _____ on the side of caution and not take unnecessary risks.

4. Archeologists often _____ ancient sites to discover artifacts.

5. His _____ explanation was confusing and unclear.

6. It was interesting to study the _____ of the dinosaurs.

7. The students _____ interest in studying abroad for a term.

8. Please _____ the requirements for the project.

9. Do not go out or you'll _____ your cold and flu.

10. He was _____ after years in prison.

11. There is a large mix of different _____ groups living in London.

12. I usually run _____ during weekends and sometimes on Tuesday.

WORD SET 18

exorbitant: [ig-SAWR-bi-tuh nt] Adjective
Exceeding the bounds of custom, propriety, or reason, especially in amount or extent.

- Minnie was surprised at the **exorbitant** fee from the bank.
- I'm trying not to make any **exorbitant** purchases because of my budget.

Synonym: extravagant, excessive, enormous, inordinate, outrageous
Antonym: cheap, good, mild
Further Information
- Originated from the Latin word *ex + orbita* meaning "out from" + "course or track."
- Should not be confused with **exuberant** meaning "full of vitality."

expeditious: [ek-spi-DISH-uh s] Adjective
Characterized by promptness.

- The assistant provided an **expeditious** answer to the questions from the managers.
- Fast food staff are used to providing **expeditious** and professional service.

Synonym: immediate, speedy, diligent, efficient, hasty
Antonym: delayed, lazy
Further Information
- Originated from the Latin word *ex + pedis* meaning "out" + "fetter or chain for feet."
- **Expeditious** implies "efficient but careful" whereas **hasty** implies "moving in speed or hurried manner."

extensive: [ik-STEN-siv] Adjective
Of great extent.
Covering or extending over a great area.

- They are planning to go on an **extensive** travel around Europe.
- The storm covered an **extensive** area over Scotland.

Synonym: thorough, broad, comprehensive, considerable, expanded
Antonym: insignificant, limited, little, miniature
Further Information
- Originated from the Latin word *ex + tendere* meaning "out" + "to stretch."
- **Extensive** may be misspelled as **extentsive** which is not a word.

extrapolate: [ik-STRAP-uh-leyt] Verb
To infer (an unknown) from something that is known.

- Data collected from one school cannot be **extrapolated** to all schools.
- The figures were **extrapolated** from past trends.

Synonym: infer, deduce, hypothesize
Antonym: doubt
Further Information
- The word was coined in 1862 by combining *extra + interpolate* meaning "outside" + "to introduce (something additional or extraneous) between other things or parts."
- In Mathematics, **extrapolate** means "extend (a graph, curve, or range of values) by inferring unknown values from trends in the known data."

extravagant: [ik-STRAV-uh-guh nt] Adjective
Spending much more than is necessary or wise.
Exceeding the bounds of reason, as actions, demands, opinions, or passions.

- He is known to be an **extravagant** fellow who spends a lot of money on unnecessary things.
- This restaurant is a little too **extravagant** for my taste.

Synonym: indulgent, wasteful, absurd, costly, exaggerated, excessive
Antonym: believable, careful, cheap
Further Information
- Originated from the Latin word *extra + vagari* meaning "outside" + "wander."
- **Extravagant** has a more negative connotation than **excessive**.

exuberance: [ig-ZOO-ber-uh ns] Noun
State of being overly excited, joyful and happy.

- Jan's **exuberance** is definitely catching and inspiring.
- The wild **exuberance** of the dancers was loved by the audience.

Synonym: energy, enthusiasm, ardor, buoyancy, eagerness
Antonym: apathy, coolness, depression
Further Information
- Originated from the Latin word *uber* meaning "fertile."
- **Exuberance** is often confused in usage with its adjective form: **exuberant**.

fallacious: [fuh-LEY-shuh s] Adjective
Containing falsehood or deception.

- Always observe **fallacious** statements during debates.
- The government may be victim to **fallacious** testimonies.

Synonym: false, wrong, deceiving, deceptive, deluding
Antonym: correct, real, accurate
Further Information
- Originated from the Latin word *fallacia* meaning "deceive."
- **Fallacious** connotes "intent to deceive."

fanatic: [fuh-NAT-ik] Noun
A person with an extreme and uncritical enthusiasm or zeal, as in religion or politics.

- Sam considers himself a fitness **fanatic** and runs every single day.
- The posters on your wall show that you're a **fanatic** supporter of the sports club.

Synonym: addict, devotee, enthusiast, extremist
Antonym: conservative, moderate
Further Information
- Originated from the Latin word *fanum* meaning "temple."
- **Fanatic** implies "extreme devotion" compared to **enthusiast** which means "a person who is interested in something."

fanatical: [fuh-NAT-i-kuh l] Adjective
Motivated or characterized by an extreme, uncritical enthusiasm or zeal, as in religion or politics.

- The **fanatical** crowd cheered for their candidate.
- When Mike was a teenager, he was a **fanatical** soccer fan.

Synonym: overenthusiastic, dogmatic, fervent, frenzied
Antonym: apathetic, calm, cool, indifferent
Further Information
- Originated from the Latin word *fanum* meaning "temple."
- Just like its noun form, **fanatic**, **fanatical** implies "extreme devotion."

fastidious: [fa-STID-ee-uh s] Adjective
Excessively particular, critical, or demanding.
Requiring or characterized by excessive care or delicacy.

- Some children prove to be **fastidious** eaters, demanding specific food.
- His boss is quite **fastidious** which adds to his worries and stress.

Synonym: meticulous, choosy, discriminating, exacting, finicky, demanding
Antonym: uncritical, undemanding, laid-back, unfussy
Further Information
- Evolved from two Latin words *fastus + taedium* meaning "contempt or arrogance" + "aversion or disgust."
- **Fastidious** implies "extreme attention to detail."

fissure: [FISH-er] Noun
A narrow opening produced by cleavage or separation of parts.

- They discovered a **fissure** on their way down the mountain.
- The earthquake created a **fissure** in the middle of the town.

Synonym: gap, cleavage, crevice, cleft
Antonym: closure, solid
Further Information
- Originated from the Latin word *findere* meaning "to split."
- A **fissure** is slightly bigger than a **crack**.

fits: [fits] Adjective/Verb/Noun
Adapted or suited. (adj.)
Fix or put (something) into place. (v.)
A sudden uncontrollable outbreak of intense emotion, laughter, coughing, or other action or activity. (n.)

- Jean **fits** the senior manager position. (adj.)
- Wait until the seamstress **fits** you in a dress. (v.)
- She was in **fits** of laughter after watching the man slip. (n.)

Synonym: suitable, appropriate, able, apt, capable
Antonym: ignorant, incapable, incompetent
Further Information
- Observed in the mid-15th century meaning "suited to the circumstances, proper."
- In Athletics, **fit** means "someone who is physically capable."

REVIEW EXERCISE 18

Match the word with its synonym.

___ 1.	exorbitant	a.	enthusiasm
___ 2.	expeditious	b.	false
___ 3.	extensive	c.	excessive
___ 4.	extrapolate	d.	gap
___ 5.	extravagant	e.	thorough
___ 6.	exuberance	f.	devotee
___ 7.	fallacious	g.	suitable
___ 8.	fanatic	h.	infer
___ 9.	fanatical	i.	demanding
___ 10.	fastidious	j.	wasteful
___ 11.	fissure	k.	speedy
___ 12.	fits	l.	overenthusiastic

From the words above, fill in the blanks with the most appropriate word. The word form may need changing.

1. Harry lives an _____ lifestyle of the rich and the famous.

2. Smith is a baseball _____ and does not miss a single game.

3. _____ scientific statements are easily spotted and disproven.

4. The _____ guest is demanding special treatment.

5. Jimmy's _____ lifts the team's spirit and inspired them to win the game.

6. The staff of the hotel was quite _____ and polite during our stay.

7. The young athlete _____ the scholarship requirements for the college team.

8. Adequate data is needed to _____ a sound conclusion.

9. He spent an _____ amount of money during the trip to Europe.

10. There is a _____ located south of the town after the earthquake.

11. Celebrities often have _____ audiences during their concerts.

12. _____ research is being conducted to find a cure for cancer.

WORD SET 19

flamboyant: [flam-BOI-uh nt] Adjective
Strikingly bold or brilliant.
Conspicuously dashing and colorful.

- His **flamboyant** performance earned a high score from the judges.
- Jimmy loves buying **flamboyant** cars and motorcycles.

Synonym: extravagant, theatrical, bombastic, brilliant, colorful
Antonym: dull, plain, simple
Further Information
- Originated from the French word *flambe* meaning "a flame."
- **Flamboyant** implies "something that is noticeable and obvious."

flannel: [FLAN-l] Noun
A soft, slightly napped fabric of wool or wool and another fiber, used for trousers, jackets, shirts, etc.

- He mostly wears **flannel** pants because of their comfort.
- **Flannel** shirts are usually popular during autumn because of their colors.

Synonym: tweed
Antonym: none
Further Information
- Originated from the Welsh word *gwlan* meaning "wool."
- **Flannel** is a type of cloth usually patterned with black and another color.

flirtatious: [flur-TEY-shuhs] Adjective
Given or inclined to amorous behavior.

- Her **flirtatious** smile is quite beautiful and endearing.
- The guy becomes **flirtatious** when the girls are around him.

Synonym: provocative, amorous
Antonym: cool, modest
Further Information
- Originated from the 1500s' word *flirt* meaning "joke or jest."
- **Flirtatious** is sometimes used informally as **flirt** or **flirty.**

florist: [FLAWR-ist] Noun
A retailer of flowers, ornamental plants, etc.

- The **florist** suggested a bouquet of roses for my girlfriend.
- During wedding season, the **florist** is very busy delivering centerpieces.

Synonym: none
Antonym: none
Further Information
- Originated from the Latin word *flos + ist* meaning "flower" + "one who does or makes."
- A **florist** is usually a business person while a **floral designer** focuses on design.

flourish: [FLUR-ish] Verb
Wave something to attract attention.
To grow luxuriantly, or thrive in growth, as a plant.

- The trees we planted last year **flourished** because of your care.
- The waitress served our food with **flourish** and flash.

Synonym: grow, thrive, embellishment, ornamentation, brandish, wave
Antonym: none
Further Information
- Originated from the Latin word *flos* meaning "flower."
- **Flourish** may also mean "to succeed or achieve something."

flowery: [FLOU-uh-ree] Adjective
Covered with or having many flowers.
(Of speech or writing) Full of elaborate words and phrases.

- The garden is **flowery** this time of the year with roses, tulips, and other beautiful blooms.
- She convinced them with **flowery** words and radiant smile.

Synonym: ornate, baroque, bombastic, embellished
Antonym: unelaborate, plain
Further Information
- Originated from the 1200s' word *flowre + -y* meaning "flower" + "full of or characterized by."
- **Flowery** is also a direct synonym of **floral**.

foliage: [FOH-lee-ij] Noun
The leaves of a plant, collectively.
The representation of leaves, flowers, and branches in paintings, architectural ornaments, etc.

- The **foliage** in the garden is getting too thick. Can you trim it a bit?
- The statue is decorated with realistic **foliage** created by skilled artists.

Synonym: leaves, vegetation, greenness
Antonym: none
Further Information
- Originated from the Latin word *folium* meaning "leaf."
- A less popular synonym for **foliage** is **leafage**.

forgery: [FAWR-juh-ree] Noun
The crime of falsely making or altering a writing by which the legal rights or obligations of another person are apparently affected.

- He was falsely accused of **forgery** by his former boss.
- **Forgery** is considered a felony in most parts of the world.

Synonym: counterfeiting, falsification
Antonym: honesty
Further Information
- Originated from the Old French word *forge + ery* meaning "smithy" + "place for."
- **Forgery** implies "a few copied objects" while **counterfeit** implies "a large number of copies."

forlorn: [fawr-LAWRN] Adjective
Desolate or dreary.
Expressive of hopelessness.

- The old house looks very **forlorn** without the family in it.
- I hate leaving every morning because my puppy looks **forlorn**.

Synonym: hopeless, depressed, deserted, desolate, desperate
Antonym: cheerful, elated, happy
Further Information
- Originated from the Old English word *for + leosan* meaning "completely" + "to lose."
- **Depressed** implies heavier emotion than **forlorn.**

forthright: [FAWRTH-rahyt] Adjective
Going straight to the point.

- It is quite a balance to be **forthright** and polite.
- The student was **forthright** in admitting that he forgot to do his homework.

Synonym: straightforward, blunt, candid, categorical, outspoken
Antonym: tactful, tricky
Further Information
- Originated from the Old English word *forth + right* meaning "forward" + "morally correct."
- **Forthright** means "being straight and honest" while **candid** implies "impartial and free from prejudice" and **offensive** means "causing resentful displeasure."

fortified: [FAWR-tuh-fahy] Verb
To protect or strengthen against attack.
To furnish with a means of resisting force or withstanding strain or wear.

- The girl was **fortified** by her faith and managed to cope with her difficulties successfully.
- The palace is **fortified** with stonewalls and wide moats.

Synonym: defended, barricaded, covered, guarded, protected
Antonym: open, unguarded
Further Information
- Originated from the Latin word *fortis* meaning "strong."
- **Fortified** can also mean "to make something better," as in breakfast cereals fortified with vitamins.

frivolous: [FRIV-uh-luh s] Adjective
Characterized by lack of seriousness or sense.
Self-indulgently carefree.

- His suggestions were **frivolous** and were ignored by the team.
- Jamie's friend did not believe her **frivolous** apology and dismissed her.

Synonym: trivial, silly, foolish, idiotic, impractical
Antonym: intelligent, sensible, wise
Further Information
- Originated from the Middle French word *fricare* meaning "to rub."
- **Frivolous** implies "not having any serious purpose or value" whereas the related word **Facetious** means "treating serious issues with deliberately inappropriate humor."

REVIEW EXERCISE 19

Match the word with its synonym.

___	1.	flamboyant	a.	wave
___	2.	flannel	b.	defended
___	3.	flirtatious	c.	provocative
___	4.	flourish	d.	trivial
___	5.	flowery	e.	depressed
___	6.	foliage	f.	extravagant
___	7.	forgery	g.	ornate
___	8.	forlorn	h.	tweed
___	9.	forthright	i.	vegetation
___	10.	fortified	j.	falsification
___	11.	frivolous	k.	blunt

From the words above, fill in the blanks with the most appropriate word. The word form may need changing.

1. There is a thick _____ growing in the garden which needed cleaning up.

2. He likes wearing _____ shirts at home for comfort.

3. With great _____, he presented the next speakers to the event.

4. Jane was _____ in her intent to be promoted and recognized.

5. His _____ words were well received by the audience.

6. _____ is a serious crime punishable by imprisonment.

7. Mindy's _____ smile is always a part of her and sets her apart from others.

8. _____ do good business on occasions like Valentine's day.

9. Theater performances are usually _____ and theatrical.

10. Harry spends a large chunk of his income on _____ purchases that he never uses.

11. The army barracks are _____ by tall walls and trees.

12. The _____ old man misses his children and family.

WORD SET 20

fundamental: [fuhn-duh-MEN-tl] Adjective/Noun
Serving as, or being an essential part of, a foundation or basis. (adj.)
A basic principle, rule, law, or the like, that serves as the groundwork of a system. (n.)

- The government is required to protect our **fundamental** rights. (adj.)
- The **fundamentals** of mathematics include arithmetic. (n.)

Synonym: basic, important, central, constitutional, crucial, elemental
Antonym: accessory, auxiliary, extrinsic
Further Information
- Originated from the Old French word *fundare* meaning "to found."
- **Fundamentals** imply "building blocks of something more advanced."

futile: [FYOO-tahyl] Adjective
Incapable of producing any result.

- His efforts proved to be **futile** which frustrated him even more.
- All defenses proved **futile** when the enemy attacked.

Synonym: hopeless, pointless, fruitless, hollow, impractical
Antonym: effective, fruitful, helpful
Further Information
- Originated from the Middle French word *futtilis* meaning "vain or worthless."
- Not to be confused with **fertile** which means "productive."

garish: [GAIR-ish] Adjective
Crudely or tastelessly colorful, showy, or elaborate, as with clothes or decoration.

- She wore **garish** clothes and obnoxious jewelry.
- They wore silly hats in **garish** colors.

Synonym: flashy, gaudy, glittering, ornate, showy
Antonym: drab, modest, plain, refined
Further Information
- Originated from the Old Norse word *gaurr* meaning "rough fellow."
- Not to be confused with **garnish** which means "to decorate (especially food)."

garment: [GAHR-muh nt] Noun
Any article of clothing. (n.)

- It is difficult to choose the correct **garment** to wear for a special party.
- I wore a waterproof outer **garment** in the rain.

Synonym: apparel, costume, dress, robe, attire
Antonym: none
Further Information
- Originated from the Old French word *garnir* meaning "equip."
- **Garment** generally refers to one item of clothing, whereas **attire** refers to all that one is wearing.

ghastly: [GAST-lee] Adjective
Shockingly frightful or dreadful.
Extremely unwell.

- He had a **ghastly** look to his face after visiting the horror house.
- Jimmy is still sick and that's why he looks **ghastly** and thin.

Synonym: horrifying, appalling, awful, frightening, frightful
Antonym: beautiful, comforting, delightful, good
Further Information
- Originated from the Old English word *gast* meaning "ghost."
- **Terrifying** implies a stronger emotion than **ghastly**.

glade: [gleyd] Noun
An open space in a forest.

- The **glade** is a perfect place to set up camp for the night.
- The boy scouts were tasked to find the **glade** in the forest.

Synonym: dell, clearing
Antonym: none
Further Information
- Originated from the Old Norse word *glaðr* meaning "bright."
- **Glen** is a secluded narrow valley compared to **glade** which is a clearing.

glib: [glib] Adjective
Readily fluent, often thoughtlessly, superficially, or insincerely so.

- Do not be **glib** about such a horrible tragedy.
- The manager is annoyed by his **glib** questions and tasteless remarks.

Synonym: slick, artful, articulate, eloquent, facile, smooth talking
Antonym: quiet, silent
<u>Further Information</u>
- Originated from the Low German word *glibberig* meaning "smooth or slippery."
- **Glib** may also mean "being talkative without careful thought."

glut: [gluht] Verb/Noun
To feed or fill to excess. (v.)
An excessive supply or amount. (n.)

- On weekends, I like to **glut** on ice cream and chocolate chip cookies. (v.)
- There is a recent **glut** of superhero films from popular comic books. (n.)

Synonym: overabundance, oversupply, saturation, surplus
Antonym: lack, need
<u>Further Information</u>
- Originated from the Latin word *gluttire* meaning "to swallow."
- A more popular noun is **glutton** which means "a person who eats and drinks excessively."

gnashed: [nash] Verb
To grind or strike (the teeth) together, especially in rage or pain.
To bite with grinding teeth.

- The hungry lions **gnashed** their teeth and lunged at the bars of the enclosure.
- He decided to **gnash** his teeth than say something mean.

Synonym: grind, clamp, crush
Antonym: none
<u>Further Information</u>
- Originated from the Danish word *knaske* meaning "crush with the teeth."
- **Gnash** is different from **gnaw** which means "to repeatedly bite something tough."

gouged: [gouj] Verb
To scoop out or hollow out.

- The sculpture was **gouged** out incorrectly which made the artist very upset.
- They tunnel was **gouged** out of the mountain.

Synonym: cut, scoop, burrow, claw
Antonym: fill
<u>Further Information</u>
- Originated from the Welsh word *gylfin* meaning "beak."
- A **gouge** is a curved blade while **chisel** is a flat blade.

governor: [GUHV-er-ner] Noun
A person charged with the direction or control of an institution, society, etc.

- The **governor** is looking forward to his first official project as a public servant.
- A new **governor** will be elected based on a popular vote next week.

Synonym: administrator, boss, chief, commander
Antonym: follower
<u>Further Information</u>
- Originated from the Greek word *kybernan* meaning "to steer or pilot a ship."
- The word **governor** is gender neutral but, sometimes, the word **governess** is used for a female governor.

gregarious: [gri-GAIR-ee-uh s] Adjective
Fond of the company of others.

- He is so **gregarious** that he becomes the life of the party.
- A **gregarious** person usually has many friends and acquaintances.

Synonym: friendly, affable, sociable
Antonym: unfriendly
<u>Further Information</u>
- Originated from the Latin word grex meaning "a flock."
- **Gregarious** implies "outgoing and comfortable with others" while **affable** means "friendly and courteous."

REVIEW EXERCISE 20

Match the word with its synonym.

___	1.	fundamental	a.	awful
___	2.	futile	b.	grind
___	3.	garish	c.	administrator
___	4.	garment	d.	scoop
___	5.	ghastly	e.	smooth-talking
___	6.	glade	f.	basic
___	7.	glib	g.	friendly
___	8.	glut	h.	gaudy
___	9.	gnash	i.	pointless
___	10.	gouged	j.	dress
___	11.	governor	k.	dell
___	12.	gregarious	l.	oversupply

From the words above, fill in the blanks with the most appropriate word. The word form may need changing.

1. Carol is a _____ child with lots of friends in school.

2. There is a beautiful _____ in the island which is popular among tourists.

3. The _____ rules of physics can be interpreted using formulas and symbols.

4. Victor's _____ remarks annoyed everyone during the meeting.

5. The tiger _____ its teeth in front of the visitors.

6. The builders _____ deep holes for the foundation of the house.

7. The house looks _____ after the loud and wild teenage party.

8. His _____ style is not envied by many.

9. The _____ helps citizens make the city better for everyone.

10. Billy saw expensive _____ in the department store.

11. All attempts to find the mythical Atlantis have been _____.

12. It is not healthy to _____ on junk food.

WORD SET 21

grovel: [GRUHV-uh l] Verb
To humble oneself or act in an abject manner, as in great fear or utter servility.
To lie or crawl with the face downward, especially in humility, fear, etc.

- He was so ashamed that he had to **grovel** and ask for favors from strangers.
- Do not **grovel** if it is not your fault or your responsibility.

Synonym: abase, demean, beseech, fawn
Antonym: ignore
Further Information
- Originated from the Old Norse *grufla* meaning "to grovel or crouch down."
- Should not be confused with **gravel** meaning "small stones and pebbles, or a mixture of these with sand."

grudging: [GRUHJ-ing] Adjective
Displaying or reflecting reluctance or unwillingness.

- Smith's **grudging** acceptance of his loss is very obvious.
- The student offered a **grudging** apology to the teacher.

Synonym: resentful, complain, covet
Antonym: allow, approve, content
Further Information
- Originated from the same word in the 15th century meaning "to murmur or complain."
- Similar to **begrudging** which means "to envy someone or to give something resentfully."

guile: [gahyl] Noun
Insidious cunning in attaining a goal; crafty or artful deception.

- Most politicians take advantage of their **guile** to convince people.
- Your **guile** will not work with your teacher anymore.

Synonym: slyness, cleverness, trickery, cunning
Antonym: frankness, honesty, honor
Further Information
- Originated from the Frankish word *wigila* meaning "trick or ruse."
- **Guile** is related but not similar to **beguile** which means "to charm or enchant (someone), sometimes in a deceptive way."

hackneyed: [hak-need] Adjective
Made commonplace or trite.

- He used the same excuse all the time and eventually it became **hackneyed**.
- Some movies have **hackneyed** plots but people still watch them.

Synonym: clichéd, tired, banal, corny, stale, trite
Antonym: fresh, new, original
Further Information
- Evolved from the figurative use of the English word *hackney* meaning "use a horse for riding."
- **Hackneyed** implies "overused" while **jaded** implies "weariness."

hallowed: [HAL-ohd] Adjective
Regarded as holy or sacred.

- The locals consider the forest as **hallowed** grounds.
- The church is taking care of **hallowed** objects for their cultural and historical value.

Synonym: holy, revered, sacred
Antonym: irreligious, unholy, unsacred
Further Information
- Originated from the Greek word *hieros* meaning "sacred or divine."
- Should not be confused with **hollowed** meaning "having a space or cavity inside."

hesitant: [hez-i-tuh nt] Adjective
Undecided, doubtful, or disinclined.

- Donna is **hesitant** to present her findings to the academic panel.
- I'm **hesitant** to tell him that he made a mistake because he's my boss.

Synonym: uncertain, waiting, afraid, averse, doubtful
Antonym: believing, bold, brace, certain, confident
Further Information
- Originated from the Latin word *haesitare* meaning "to stick fast and stammer."
- **Hesitant** implies "unsure but willing" while **reluctant** means "unsure but unwilling."

hoist: [hoist] Verb/Noun
To raise or lift, especially by some mechanical appliance. (v.)
An apparatus for hoisting, as a block and tackle, a derrick, or a crane. (n.)

- I really don't know how to **hoist** this couch to the second floor. (v.)
- I think the **hoist** holding the flag is broken. (n.)

Synonym: lift, erect, heave, pick up
Antonym: abandon, decrease, depress
Further Information
- Originated from the Old Norse word *hissa upp* meaning "raise."
- **Hoist** implies "raising something using a machine" while **lift** is a general term for "moving to a higher place."

horrific: [haw-RIF-ik] Adjective
Causing horror or fear.

- There was a **horrific** accident across town which caused heavy traffic.
- Performing in front of the crowd is not so **horrific** after all.

Synonym: horrible, abominable, appalling, awful, cruel
Antonym: attractive, beautiful, delightful, gentle
Further Information
- Originated from the Latin word *horrere* meaning "tremble or shudder."
- Should not be confused with **honorific** meaning "conveying honor."

humble: [HUHM-buh l] Adjective/Verb
Not proud or arrogant. (adj.)
To lower in condition, importance, or dignity. (v.)

- He is known to be a **humble** fellow with a big heart. (adj.)
- After such actions, he **humbled** himself to regain trust from people. (v.)

Synonym: meek, unassuming, courteous, gentle, modest
Antonym: bold, brave, complex, complicated, discourteous
Further Information
- Originated from the Latin *humilis* meaning "lowly or humble."
- Being **humble** means "acknowledging one's strength while being comfortable with another's authority" while **modest** means "not showing off."

humid: [HYOO-mid] Adjective
Containing a high amount of water or water vapor.

- The weather is very **humid** when it's cloudy and the temperature is high.
- It's usually **humid** in tropical areas during summer.

Synonym: damp, dank, moist, muggy, oppressive
Antonym: cold, cool, dehydrated
Further Information
- Originated from the Latin word *humere* meaning "be moist."
- **Humid** is the "presence of water in the air" while **hot** implies "high temperature."

impending: [im-PEN-ding] Adjective
About to happen.
Imminently threatening or menacing.

- I feel like there's an **impending** danger in this trip.
- There is an **impending** storm from the south as evident from the dark clouds.

Synonym: forthcoming, approaching, brewing, imminent, looming
Antonym: gone, past
Further Information
- Originated from the Latin word *in + pendere* meaning "forward" + "hang."
- Should not be confused with **pending** meaning "awaiting decision."

impenetrable: [im-PEN-i-truh-buh l] Adjective
That which cannot be penetrated, pierced, entered, etc.
Inaccessible to ideas, influences, etc.

- The castle is practically **impenetrable** thanks to the walls and the cavalry.
- His confidence is **impenetrable** even during difficult times.

Synonym: dense, bulletproof, impassable, impervious
Antonym: open, penetrable
Further Information
- Originated from the Latin word *in + penetrabilis* meaning "opposite of" + "penetrable."
- **Impenetrable** implies" that which cannot be penetrated from the outside" while **impregnable** means "unable to be defeated."

REVIEW EXERCISE 21

Match the word with its synonym.

___	1.	grovel	a.	revered
___	2.	grudging	b.	cunning
___	3.	guile	c.	damp
___	4.	hackneyed	d.	lift
___	5.	hallowed	e.	uncertain
___	6.	hesitant	f.	impassable
___	7.	hoist	g.	resentful
___	8.	horrific	h.	forthcoming
___	9.	humble	i.	demean
___	10.	humid	j.	clichéd
___	11.	impending	k.	abominable
___	12.	impenetrable	l.	modest

From the words above, fill in the blanks with the most appropriate word. The word form may need changing.

1. He had a sense of _____ doom while entering the haunted house.

2. Scientists are developing _____ body suits that can withstand bullets.

3. His _____ effort shows that he is not willing to do the task at hand.

4. In the tropics, it is often _____ and hot during summer.

5. The book's plot was _____ and the children struggled to finish reading it.

6. The dog was willing to_____ for the bone.

7. I love children's innocence and lack of _____.

8. The mountain is considered _____ area by the ethic residents.

9. Many millionaires are self-made and come from a_____ background.

10. Cranes are used to _____ heavy materials at construction sites.

11. Howard is _____ to dive from such height.

12. The _____ accident affected many people and properties.

WORD SET 22

imperative: [im-PER-uh-tiv] Adjective/Noun
Absolutely necessary or required. (adj.)
A command. (n.)

- It is **imperative** to clean up after using the gymnasium. (adj.)
- It is an **imperative** to keep good relationships among nations. (n.)

Synonym: necessary, critical, crucial, essential, immediate
Antonym: inessential, insignificant, optional
Further Information
- Originated from the Late Latin word *in + parare* meaning "toward" + "make ready."
- Should not be confused with **imperial** meaning "pertaining to an empire."

imperious: [im-PEER-ee-uh s] Adjective
Domineering in a haughty manner.
Urgent or needed.

- The president has an **imperious** manner which intimidates his staff.
- The Queen raised her hand in an **imperious** manner and signaled the end of discussion.

Synonym: bossy, overbearing, arrogant, haughty, tyrannical
Antonym: democratic, humble, meek
Further Information
- Originated from the Latin word *in + parare* meaning "in" + "to order or prepare."
- Should not be confused with **impervious** meaning "not permitting penetration or passage."

impetuous: [im-PECH-oo-uh s] Adjective
Of, relating to, or characterized by sudden or rash action, emotion, etc.

- He regretted his **impetuous** decision to buy a sports car.
- It's easy to be **impetuous** when you're young and carefree.

Synonym: rash, hasty, reckless, impulsive
Antonym: calm, cautious
Further Information
- Originated from the Latin word *in + petere* meaning "into" + "aim for."
- Being **impetuous** implies **carelessness**.

impish: [IM-pish] Adjective
To be mischievous.
Acting in a childish way like a rascal.

- Do not act like an **impish** child and wreak havoc during class.
- His **impish** attitude is quite adorable but sometimes annoying.

Synonym: mischievous, devilish, jaunty, naughty, playful
Antonym: good, moral
Further Information
- Originated from the Old English *impa + ish* meaning "young shoot" + "native of something."
- **Impish** implies "doing naughty things for fun" while **mischievous** implies "being troublesome."

implicate: [IM-pli-keyt] Verb
To show someone to be involved in a crime.

- The witness **implicated** an innocent person in the crime.
- He had been **implicated** in a financial scandal.

Synonym: imply, involve, accuse, affect, blame
Antonym: exclude, exculpate, exonerate, praise
Further Information
- Originated from the Latin word *in + plicare* meaning "into" + "to fold."
- **Implicate** implies "involving something that results in consequence" while **imply** means "conveying something without explicitly stating it."

implore: [im-PLAWR] Verb
To beg urgently or piteously for (aid, mercy, pardon, etc.)

- They **implored** him to work for the company after he showed how skillful he was.
- The beggar **implored** for a little change so he could eat.

Synonym: beg, beseech, plead, pray, urge
Antonym: refuse
Further Information
- Originated from the Middle French word *in + plorare* meaning "upon" + "to weep or cry out."
- A variant spelling is **emplore**.

inadvertent: [in-uh d-VUR-tnt] Adjective
Something unintentional.
Of, relating to, or characterized by lack of attention.

- An **inadvertent** blessing came to the family in the form of three puppies.
- The microwave is an **inadvertent** invention which resulted in a successful business.

Synonym: accidental, careless, reckless, unintended, unintentional
Antonym: careful, cautious, intentional
Further Information
- Originated from the Latin word *in + advertentia* meaning "not" + "to direct one's attention."
- **Inadvertent** implies "resulting from something unplanned" whereas **accident** means "an unfortunate incident."

inattentive: [in-uh-TEN-tiv] Adjective
Not attentive; negligent.

- After more than four hours of class, I become **inattentive** because of tiredness.
- It is difficult to teach **inattentive** students especially when the topic is not that interesting.

Synonym: negligent, apathetic, careless, distracted, distraught
Antonym: caring, concerned, interested
Further Information
- Originated from the Latin word *in + attendere* meaning "opposite of" + "give heed to."
- **Inattentive** means "to lose interest" while **distracted** implies "inability to focus."

indeterminate: [in-di-TUR-muh-nit] Adjective
Not defined; not precisely fixed in extent.

- Mark spent an **indeterminate** amount of money in the festival looking for interesting dishes to try.
- There is an **indeterminate** number of birds feeding in the park.

Synonym: uncertain, vague, undetermined
Antonym: certain, definite
Further Information
- Originated from the Late Latin *in + deteminatus* meaning "not" + "limited."
- In Mathematics, **indeterminate** means "something whose value is not specified."

indispensable: [in-di-SPEN-suh-buh l] Adjective
Absolutely necessary, essential, or requisite.
A person or thing that is indispensable.

- Everyone in the team is **indispensable** because of their expertise.
- The textbook is an **indispensable** part of learning.

Synonym: necessary, basic, crucial, essential, fundamental
Antonym: additional, auxiliary, extra, inessential
Further Information
- Originated from the Latin word *in + dispensabilis* meaning "opposite of" + "disburse or administer."
- **Indispensable** is commonly misspelled as **indispensible**.

indulge: [in-DUHLJ] Verb
To yield to an inclination or desire.
To yield to, satisfy, or gratify (desires, feelings, etc.)

- I sometimes **indulge** in an extra serving of dessert when I'm feeling down.
- Janet sometimes **indulges** in luxury spending like buying jewelry and bags.

Synonym: entertain, nourish, pamper, satiate, satisfy
Antonym: deprive, dissatisfy. neglect
Further Information
- Originated from the Latin word *indulgere* meaning "to give free reign to."
- **Indulge** may imply "to fully follow one's desire."

industrious: [in-DUHS-tree-uh s] Adjective
Working energetically and devotedly; hard-working.

- Johnny is known to be a very **industrious** and smart worker.
- If you are **industrious** enough, you can finish college in three years instead of four.

Synonym: hardworking, conscientious, diligent, energetic
Antonym: inactive, lazy, lethargic
Further Information
- Originated from the Latin word *in + struere* meaning "within" + "to build."
- Should not be confused with **industria**l meaning "of, pertaining to, of the nature of, or resulting from industry."

REVIEW EXERCISE 22

Match the word with its synonym.

___	1.	imperative	a.	critical
___	2.	imperious	b.	impulsive
___	3.	impetuous	c.	beg
___	4.	impish	d.	accidental
___	5.	implicate	e.	apathetic
___	6.	implore	f.	arrogant
___	7.	inadvertent	g.	necessary
___	8.	inattentive	h.	vague
___	9.	indeterminate	i.	satiate
___	10.	indispensable	j.	mischievous
___	11.	indulge	k.	involve
___	12.	industrious	l.	diligent

From the words above, fill in the blanks with the most appropriate word. The word form may need changing.

1. The _____ cook burned the food and almost caused a fire.

2. The _____ result of the experiment meant that it had to be repeated carefully.

3. It is _____ for students to study for the exams.

4. The leader has an _____ attitude that the members don't like.

5. The _____ child was boisterous during the class.

6. Billy is an _____ employee that's why the company won't let him go.

7. Johnny _____ deleted important files in his computer.

8. The suspect was _____ in the crime after the witnesses came forward.

9. Noel's _____ decision to buy an expensive car put him in huge debt.

10. I often _____ in tubs of ice cream when I'm sad.

11. Lewis is an _____ student who always gets top grades.

12. Parents _____ their children to study for the test.

WORD SET 23

inedible: [in-ED-uh-buh l] Adjective
Unfit to be eaten.

- Make sure that you're not collecting **inedible** mushrooms or else we'll get poisoned.
- Jan put so much hot sauce in her dish that it has become **inedible**.

Synonym: unpalatable, uneatable
Antonym: eatable
Further Information
- Originated from the Late Latin word *in + edibilis* meaning "opposite of" + "eatable."
- **Inedible** is commonly misspelled as **unedible**.

inevitable: [in-ev-i-tuh-buh l] Adjective/Noun
Unable to be avoided, evaded, or escaped from. (adj.)
That which is unavoidable. (n.)

- Getting old is something **inevitable** that we all have to face. (adj.)
- Global warming becomes **inevitable** as we continue ignoring it. (n.)

Synonym: certain, imminent, impending, inescapable, inexorable, unavoidable
Antonym: avoidable, escapable, later
Further Information
- Originated from the Latin word *in + evitare* meaning "not" + "avoid."
- The synonym **imminent** implies stronger emotion as it connotes "looming or threatening."

inherent: [in-HER-uh nt] Adjective
Existing in someone or something as a permanent and inseparable element, quality, or attribute.

- His **inherent** creativity allowed him to apply for art school.
- Despite his **inherent** fear of mathematics, he worked hard to get straight A's.

Synonym: basic, built-in, deep-rooted, deep-seated, essential
Antonym: acquired, auxiliary, extra, extrinsic
Further Information
- Originated from the Latin word *in + harere* meaning "in" + "to stick."
- **Inherent** implies "something that comes naturally" while **intrinsic** implies "something that can be acquired."

innocuous: [ih-NOK-yoo-uh s] Adjective
Not harmful or injurious.
Not likely to irritate or offend.

- Drinking lemon tea when you have a cold is an **innocuous** home remedy.
- Lea makes sure that she appears **innocuous** and polite.

Synonym: harmless, banal, bland, inoffensive, insipid, painless
Antonym: harmful, obnoxious
Further Information
- Originated from the Latin word *in + nocuss* meaning "not" + "injurious."
- Should not be confused with **innocent** meaning "free from moral wrong."

insulate: [IN-suh-leyt] Verb
To cover, line, or separate with a material that prevents or reduces the passage, transfer, or leakage of heat, electricity, or sound.
To protect from unpleasant influences or experiences.

- The rubber coating **insulates** the wires to prevent short circuits.
- Sometimes, Jan **insulates** herself from a situation to avoid becoming emotional.

Synonym: protect, cushion, seclude, sequester, shield, wrap
Antonym: join, mingle, uncover
Further Information
- Originated from the Latin word *insula + ate* meaning "island" + a verb forming suffix.
- Similar to **isolated** meaning "to set apart from a group."

insurmountable: [in-ser-MOUN-tuh-buh l] Adjective
Incapable of being surmounted, passed over, or overcome.

- Sometimes, problems seem **insurmountable** when you're stressed out.
- He overcame **insurmountable** situations to succeed in life.

Synonym: impossible, hopeless, impassable, impregnable, invincible
Antonym: beatable, surmountable
Further Information
- Originated from the 1600s' French word i*n + sur + monter* meaning "opposite" + "beyond" + "to go up."
- **Insurmountable** is commonly misspelled as **unsurmountable**.

integrate: [IN-ti-greyt] Verb
To bring together or incorporate (parts) into a whole.
To make up, combine, or complete to produce a whole or a larger unit.

- It was a bit challenging to **integrate** into the new neighborhood.
- You need to **integrate** the result of your first and second experiment.

Synonym: mix, merge, accommodate, blend
Antonym: disarrange, disconnect, disjoin, disperse
Further Information
- Originated from the Latin word *in + tangere* meaning "not" + "to touch."
- **Integrate** implies "incorporating an individual to a group" while **assimilate** means "to adopt the ways of another culture or group."

integrity: [in-TEG-ri-tee] Noun
Adherence to moral and ethical principles; soundness of moral character; honesty.

- Lewis tries to live with **integrity** every day.
- **Integrity** is sometimes hard to find in people these days.

Synonym: honor, uprightness, honesty, principle, probity
Antonym: deceit, dishonesty
Further Information
- Originated from the Latin word *in + tangere* meaning "not" + "to touch."
- **Integrity** implies "adherence to a standard" while **virtue** is having "high moral standards."

intermittently: [in-ter-MIT-nt-lee] Adverb
Stopping or ceasing for a time; alternately ceasing and beginning again.

- The power kept going off **intermittently** during the storm.
- They **intermittently** see each other during the week.

Synonym: occasionally, periodically, irregularly
Antonym: constantly, continuously
Further Information
- Originated from the Latin word *inter + mittere* meaning "between" + "let go."
- **Intermittently** implies "stopping and starting at intervals" while **sporadically** means "rare and scattered in occurrence."

interval: [IN-ter-vuh l] Noun
An intervening period of time.
A space between things, points, limits, etc.

- The **interval** between semesters can be used to work part-time.
- The rapids have short **intervals** of still water.

Synonym: break, pause, interruption, lull
Antonym: continuation
Further Information
- Originated from the Latin word *inter + vallum* meaning "between" + "rampart."
- **Interval** is often used to refer to time and space.

introvert: [IN-truh-vurt] Noun/Adjective/Verb
A shy person. (n.)
A mark of introversion. (adj.)
To turn inward. (v.)

- He's naturally an **introvert**, so he loves to stay at home and relax. (n.)
- His **introvert** nature makes it hard for him to socialize during parties. (adj.)
- Sometimes I have to **introvert** my thoughts before speaking out. (v.)

Synonym: shy, brooder, loner
Antonym: none
Further Information
- Originated from the Modern Latin word *intro + vertere* meaning "to the inside" + "to turn."
- **Introvert** implies "preference for quiet environment" while **shy** means "fear of negative judgment."

invigorated: [in-VIG-uh-reyt d] Verb
To give vigor to; fill with life and energy.

- The rain **invigorated** the otherwise dry soil, so the plants grew.
- He felt **invigorated** from drinking lemonade after playing under the hot sun.

Synonym: stimulated, energized, enlivened, excited, quickened
Antonym: bored, destroyed, discouraged, dissuaded
Further Information
- Originated from the 1600s' word *in + vigor + ate* meaning "opposite of" + "energy in activity" + verbal suffix.

REVIEW EXERCISE 23

Match the word with its synonym.

___	1.	inedible	a.	wrap
___	2.	inevitable	b.	harmless
___	3.	inherent	c.	unavoidable
___	4.	innocuous	d.	break
___	5.	insulate	e.	honor
___	6.	insurmountable	f.	impossible
___	7.	integrate	g.	unpalatable
___	8.	integrity	h.	deep-rooted
___	9.	intermittently	i.	periodically
___	10.	interval	j.	shy
___	11.	introvert	k.	merge
___	12.	invigorated	l.	energized

From the words above, fill in the blanks with the most appropriate word. The word form may need changing.

1. The small lamb seemed_____but gave a hard kick if you got too close.

2. Receiving good grades is _____ if you work hard.

3. Leo's _____ is admired by everyone because he refuses to compromise on

   matters of principle.

4. Lightning _____ appears during thunderstorms.

5. The _____ between TV shows are filled with commercials.

6. Her _____ talent helped her bloom as a professional singer.

7. Expired foods are _____ and sometimes poisonous.

8. It is challenging to _____into a new country, especially when you move when older.

9. He feels _____ from taking a bath after getting home from work.

10. Wear thick clothes during winter to _____ yourself from the cold.

11. Ben is typically _____ and shy.

12. Some trials and challenges may seem _____ sometimes.

WORD SET 24

invoke: [in-vohk] Verb
To call for with earnest desire.
To declare to be binding in effect.

- The leader **invoked** the support of all the team members.
- Any citizen can **invoke** their rights as stated in the country's constitution.

Synonym: call upon, appeal to, conjure
Antonym: answer, reply
<u>Further Information</u>
- Originated from the Latin word *in + vocare* meaning "upon" + "to call."
- Should not be confused with **evoke** which means "to draw forth to mind, usually feelings and emotions."

ire: [ahyuh r] Noun
Intense anger.

- Do not show your **ire** to the public as it can make them uncomfortable.
- Make sure to finish all your tasks or you'll earn the **ire** of the manager.

Synonym: anger, annoyance, displease, fury, indignation
Antonym: calm, comfort, delight, joy
<u>Further Information</u>
- Originated from the Latin word *ira* meaning "anger."
- The synonyms **wrath** and **fury** evoke stronger emotions than **ire**.

jaded: [jey-did] Adjective
Dulled or satiated by over-indulgence.
Worn out or wearied.

- It's just the 3rd class and he already feels **jaded**.
- The employee tried out new things to avoid feeling **jaded**.

Synonym: exhausted, bored, tired, weary
Antonym: excited, fresh, activated
<u>Further Information</u>
- Evolved from the Old Norse word *jalda* meaning "horse."
- **Jaded** implies "a combination of exhaustion and boredom."

jaunt: [jawnt] Noun/Verb
A short journey. (n.)
To make a short journey. (v.)

- Having a fun **jaunt** with your friends is always great. (n.)
- My **jaunt** to the grocery store is usually uneventful. (v.)

Synonym: expedition, excursion, jog, journey, junket
Antonym: none
Further Information
- Became popular in the 1500s and meant "tire (a horse) by riding back and forth."
- Unrelated to the adjective **jaunty** which means "having or expressing a lively, cheerful, and self-confident manner."

jeer: [jeer] Verb/Noun
To speak or shout derisively. (v.)
A rude or mocking remark. (n.)

- The home crowd **jeered** at the opponent during the game. (v.)
- A lot of his coworkers did not appreciate his **jeers** during the meeting. (n.)

Synonym: heckle, hoot, quip, ridicule, scoff
Antonym: compliment, praise
Further Information
- Originated from the 1500s' word *gyr* meaning "deride or mock."
- **Jeer** implies "loud negative remarks" while **heckle** implies "harsh utterance in an attempt to find weakness."

jeopardy: [JEP-er-dee] Noun
Hazard or risk of or exposure to loss, harm, death, or injury.

- Cops put their lives in **jeopardy** on a daily basis.
- Do not put yourself in **jeopardy** by taking a selfie on a cliff.

Synonym: danger, trouble, peril
Antonym: assurance, certainty
Further Information
- Originated from the Old French phrase *ieu parti* meaning "evenly divided game."
- In Law, **jeopardy** means "danger of being convicted and punished for a criminal offence."

jibe: [jahyb] Verb/Noun
To be in harmony or accord. (v.)
To utter mocking or scoffing words. (n.)

- The new student **jibed** with the rest of the class quickly. (v.)
- Frequent **jibes**, however gentle, can be very annoying. (n.)

Synonym: conform, correspond, dovetail, harmonize, agree, match
Antonym: differ, disagree, fight
Further Information
- Originated from the English word *gybe* meaning "shift a sail or boom."
- **Jibe** can be spelled as **gibe** and **jibb**.

juxtaposed: [juhk-stuh-pohz] Verb
To place close together or side by side, typically in comparison.

- **Juxtaposed** against the sad tragedy are the stories of heroism.
- The artist **juxtaposed** the beauty of colors and the elegance of white and black in his recent work.

Synonym: connected, paired, compared, adjacent
Antonym: none
Further Information
- Originated from the combination of the Latin word *juxta* and the French word *poser* which means "next" + "poser."
- **Juxtaposed** implies "nearness between the objects" while **comparison** is "to examine objects against each other."

lackluster: [lak-luhs-ter] Adjective
Lacking brilliance or radiance.
A lack of brilliance or vitality.

- There were no excuses for the team's **lackluster** performance.
- Due to the slowing economy, the company's profits were **lackluster**.

Synonym: dull, lifeless, boring, flat, muted
Antonym: bright, exciting, lively
Further Information
- Originated from the Old English word *lac* and the Middle French word *lustre* meaning "lack of" + "gloss or radiance."
- Spelled as **lacklustre** in British English.

landmark: [land-mahrk] Noun/Verb
A prominent or conspicuous object on land that serves as a guide. (n.)
To declare (a building, site, etc.) a landmark. (v.)

- The valley is a known **landmark** in the area. (n.)
- UNESCO **landmarked** many natural treasures. (v.)

Synonym: marker, memorial, milestone, monument
Antonym: whole
Further Information
- Originated from the Old English word *land + mearc* meaning "ground or soil" + "boundary or sign."
- A **landmark** may also mean "something significant, note-worthy, or important."
  For example, "A landmark achievement."

languid: [lang-gwid] Adjective
Lacking in vigor or vitality.
Lacking in spirit or interest.

- Her **languid** reply tells me that she is not interested in traveling alone.
- After a long day, the waiter moved in a **languid** manner.

Synonym: drooping, lazy, leisurely, lethargic
Antonym: energetic, lively
Further Information
- Originated from the Middle French word *languere* meaning "weak or fatigued."
- **Languid** implies "lacking in energy due to exhaustion."

languish: [lang-gwish] Verb
To be or become weak or feeble.
Fail to make progress.

- Jamie's project **languished** on his desk for weeks.
- The plants **languished** and died from the drought.

Synonym: droop, deteriorate, dwindle, fail, weaken
Antonym: build, develop, grow
Further Information
- Originated from the Latin word *languere* meaning "be weak or faint."
- Should not be confused with **languid** meaning "lacking in vigor or vitality."

REVIEW EXERCISE 24

Match the word with its synonym.

___	1.	invoke	a.	monument
___	2.	ire	b.	tired
___	3.	jaded	c.	droop
___	4.	jaunt	d.	hoot
___	5.	jeer	e.	anger
___	6.	jeopardy	f.	leisurely
___	7.	jibe	g.	adjacent
___	8.	juxtaposed	h.	lifeless
___	9.	lackluster	i.	agree
___	10.	landmark	j.	call upon
___	11.	languid	k.	trouble
___	12.	languish	l.	expedition

From the words above, fill in the blanks with the most appropriate word. The word form may need changing.

1. Do not earn the _____ of your friends by making fun of them.

2. The actor's _____ performance was not well received.

3. Eiffel Tower is a popular French _____ visited by many tourists.

4. _____ against the dark backgrounds is an elegant statue.

5. Smith _____ his rights to have his lawyer present before he made a statement.

6. The _____ movement of the snake indicated that it was probably not going to attack.

7. I am a good listener and can _____ with a wide variety of people.

8. The audience _____ during the theater performance because they disliked the show.

9. Victor _____ in bed for a few days because of flu.

10. His _____ to the nearby mountain was adventurous yet relaxing.

11. You career will be in _____ if you don't do your best and meet expectations.

12. This has been a long tiring week and I am feeling quite _____.

WORD SET 25

laud: [lawd] Verb
To praise.

- Sunny was **lauded** during her graduation for her academic achievements.
- The new single was **lauded** by the music press.

Synonym: acclaim, admire, adore, celebrate, commend
Antonym: abhor, blame, censure, condemn
Further Information
- Originated from the Latin word *laus* meaning "praise."
- Should not be confused with **loud** meaning "strongly audible."

lethargic: [luh-THAHR-jik] Adjective
Of, relating to, or affected with sluggishness.

- The hot weather makes me **lethargic** and sleepy.
- Walking all these flights of stairs make me **lethargic** and out of breath.

Synonym: lazy, apathetic, dull, laid-back, listless
Antonym: active, alert, animated
Further Information
- Originated from the Greek word *lethargikos* meaning "drowsy."
- **Lethargic** implies "sleepiness or drowsiness."

liberate: [LIB-uh-reyt] Verb
To set free, as from imprisonment or bondage.

- South Sudan was **liberated** only recently, so it is a very young country.
- I feel **liberated** after school when I can play football.

Synonym: detach, emancipate, free, redeem, rescue
Antonym: harm, hold, hurt, detain
Further Information
- Originated from the Latin word *liber* meaning "free."
- In Chemistry and Physics, **liberate** means "release (gas, energy, etc.) as a result of chemical reaction or physical decomposition."

liberation: [lib-uh-REY-shuh n] Noun
The act of setting someone free.
The act or fact of gaining equal rights or full social or economic opportunities for a particular group.

- A country's **liberation** is the start of the difficult journey to independence.
- The citizens celebrated their **liberation** from the colonizers.

Synonym: freedom, abolition, deliverance, democracy
Antonym: none
Further Information
- Originated from the Latin word *liber* meaning "free."

liveliness: [LAHYV-lee-nes] Noun
Full or suggestive of life or vital energy.
The quality of being animated, spirited, vivacious, or sprightly.

- I always enjoy the teacher's **liveliness** during a class.
- Joanna's **liveliness** shows in her smile and laughter.

Synonym: animation, action, energy, vitality
Antonym: idle, lazy, lethargy
Further Information
- Originated from the Old English word *lif + ly + ness* meaning "animated" + a suffix for adjectives.
- Sometimes misspelled as **livelyness** which is not a word.

lodging: [LOJ-ing] Noun
Accommodation in a house, especially in rooms for rent.

- Have you arranged our **lodging** for the camping trip?
- This **lodging** is very luxurious with many high-end amenities.

Synonym: accommodation, apartment, hostel, hotel, inn
Antonym: none
Further Information
- Originated from the Old French word *loge* meaning "hut."
- **Lodging** implies "temporary home or house."
- **Boarding** as in Lodging & Boarding, implies "receiving regular meals for payment."

lout: [lout] Noun/Verb
Uncouth or aggressive man or boy. (n.)
To bow in respect. (v.)

- Sometimes, he can be such a **lout** when disturbed. (n.)
- Everyone should **lout** once the queen passes by. (v.)

Synonym: boor, brute, buffoon, ruffian, rowdy, slob
Antonym: gentleman
Further Information
- Originated from the Middle English word *louten* meaning "bow down."
- Should not be confused with **loot** which means "to rob."

lucrative: [loo-kruh-tiv] Adjective
Profitable or money-making.

- They say business in real estate is very **lucrative**.
- He is working hard to put up a business in the **lucrative** part of town.

Synonym: productive, advantageous, fruitful, moneymaking
Antonym: unprofitable
Further Information
- Originated from the Latin word *lucrum* meaning "gain or profit."
- **Lucrative** connotes "gaining a lot with not much effort."
- Related word **lucre** means "money/wealth."

lurid: [LUR-id] Adjective
Gruesome; horrible.
Glaringly vivid or sensational.

- It was quite uncomfortable to hear the **lurid** details of the accident.
- The **lurid** gossip is the talk of the town, but it is untrue.

Synonym: shocking, gruesome, exaggerated, ghastly, gory
Antonym: clean, delightful, dull, mild
Further Information
- Originated from the Latin word *luror* meaning "wan or yellow."
- **Lurid** implies "fine details or account" while **vivid** implies "visual details."

magistrate: [MAJ-uh-streyt] Noun
A civil officer charged with the administration of the law.

- The **magistrate** summoned the witnesses to the accident.
- He is known to be a fair but strict **magistrate**.

Synonym: civil officer, bailiff, judge
Antonym: *none*
<u>Further Information</u>
- Evolved from the Latin word *magister* meaning "master."
- **Magistrate** is typically a public official.

malicious: [muh-LISH-uh s] Adjective
Full of, characterized by, or showing ill-will; intentionally harmful.

- Do not believe all the **malicious** rumors going around town.
- I'm not sure if he has **malicious** intent or he was just unaware of his actions.

Synonym: hateful, malevolent, malignant, mischievous, nasty
Antonym: decent, friendly, gentle, good, harmless
<u>Further Information</u>
- Originated from the Latin word *malus* meaning "bad or unpleasant."
- In Law, **malicious** means "vicious, wanton, or mischievous in motivation or purpose."
- Other words with **mal** as a prefix are: *Malaise, Malady, Maleficence, Malice* etc. All of these words have a negative connotation.

malign: [muh-LAHYN] Verb/Adjective
To speak harmful untruths about. (v.)
Having or showing an evil disposition. (adj.)

- It is not honorable to **malign** another person. (v.)
- The dark colors and dull furniture create a **maligned** atmosphere. (adj.)

Synonym: hurtful, injurious, antagonistic, defame, slander
Antonym: aiding, benign, helpful
<u>Further Information</u>
- Originated from the Latin word *malus* meaning "bad."
- The adjective form of **malign** is **malignant** meaning "disposed to cause harm, suffering, or distress deliberately."

REVIEW EXERCISE 25

Match the word with its synonym.

___ 1.	laud	a.	money-making
___ 2.	lethargic	b.	admire
___ 3.	liberate	c.	vitality
___ 4.	liberation	d.	defame
___ 5.	liveliness	e.	shocking
___ 6.	lodging	f.	bailiff
___ 7.	lout	g.	lazy
___ 8.	lucrative	h.	emancipate
___ 9.	lurid	i.	brute
___ 10.	magistrate	j.	freedom
___ 11.	malicious	k.	accommodation
___ 12.	malign	l.	malevolent

From the words above, fill in the blanks with the most appropriate word. The word form may need changing.

1. Garfield the cat was _____ today because of his illness.

2. Sometimes celebrities are _____ with untrue rumors.

3. Jamie's _____ nightmare woke her up feeling terrified.

4. The _____ they stayed at in Japan was full of tourists.

5. Phoebe's _____ makes her the life of the party.

6. Some _____ websites can infect your computer with viruses.

7. It felt _____ when I left for a vacation after working non-stop for six months.

8. Charlie is the neighborhood _____ and everyone tries to avoid him.

9. A business in IT can be quite _____ and rewarding.

10. Professor Adams was _____ as the best in his field.

11. Countries _____ from their colonizers often work hard to rebuild their national pride.

12. The _____ can be quite strict in implementing the law.

WORD SET 26

maltreat: [mal-TREET] Verb
To treat or handle badly, cruelly, or roughly.

- The company is careful not to **maltreat** its employees.
- You should never **maltreat** someone who is weaker than you.

Synonym: abuse, victimize, damage
Antonym: aid, assist, benefit
<u>Further Information</u>
- Originated from the 1700s' word *mal + treat* meaning "bad or ill" + "action."
- Another form of **maltreat** is mistreat.

marquee: [mahr-KEE] Noun/Adjective
A large tent used for functions; A tall roof like projection above a theater entrance or gymnasium. (n.)
Leading; Pre-eminent. (adj.)

- The **marquee** was large enough to accommodate the whole team. (n.)
- They welcomed the **marquee** player from the game. (adj.)

Synonym: canopy, awning, signboard
Antonym: none
<u>Further Information</u>
- Originated from the French word *marquise* meaning "linen canopy over a tent."
- Should not be confused with **marque** meaning "a product model or type, as of a luxury or racing car."

memorandum: [mem-uh-RAN-duh m] Noun
A short note designating something to be remembered.

- We are still waiting for the president to sign the **memorandum**.
- Have you read the **memorandum** about the new dress code?

Synonym: note, announcement, diary, directive, letter
Antonym: none
<u>Further Information</u>
- Originated from the Latin word *memor* meaning "mindful of."
- In Law, **memorandum** means "a piece of writing, usually informal, containing the terms of a transaction." As in *Memorandum of Understanding (MoU)* for the sale of a public company.

merciless: [MUR-si-lis] Adjective
Having or showing no compassion; Cruel.

- The decision was quite **merciless** for me, as it was very strict.
- Minny is considered a **merciless** debater because she can take on anyone.

Synonym: mean, heartless, barbarous, callous, cruel
Antonym: compassionate, considerate, merciful
Further Information
- Originated from the Middle English word *merci + less* meaning "pity" + "lacking/cannot be."
- **Merciless** connotes "cruel attitude" while **mean** connotes "to be unkind."

meritorious: [mer-i-TAWR-ee-uh s] Adjective
Deserving praise, reward, esteem, etc.

- At such a young age, he has many **meritorious** achievements.
- Even with a second place, his win still feels **meritorious**.

Synonym: honorable, commendable, exemplary, praiseworthy
Antonym: corrupt, dishonorable
Further Information
- Originated from the Old French word *merite + ous* meaning "wages, pay or reward" + suffix making adjectives.
- Should not be confused with **meretricious** meaning "alluring by a show of flashy or vulgar attractions."

meticulous: [muh-TIK-yuh-luh s] Adjective
Taking or showing extreme care about minute details.

- It is fascinating to see her **meticulous** attention to detail.
- The **meticulous** design gives an air of elegance to the statue.

Synonym: detailed, perfectionist, accurate, cautious, precise
Antonym: careless, false, imprecise, inaccurate, indefinite
Further Information
- Originated from the Latin word *metus* meaning "fear."
- **Meticulous** means "careful attention to detail" while **fastidious** means "fussy about details."

mews: [myoos] Noun
A yard or street lined by buildings originally used as stables but now often converted into dwellings.

- The house is located in a faraway **mews** outside the city limits.
- She bought a **mews** house outside London to avoid the crowded streets.

Synonym: alley, close, lance
Antonym: None
Further Information
- Originated from the Old English word *mæw* meaning "seagull."
- **Mews** can also mean "the sound a cat makes."

minuscule: [MIN-uh-skyool] Adjective/Noun
Very small. (adj.)
A small or lower case letter. (n.)

- Even a **minuscule** donation can help the charity set up a scholarship program. (adj.)
- The old book is full of **minuscules** which can be very hard to read. (n.)

Synonym: insignificant, microscopic, small, tiny
Antonym: big, enormous, huge
Further Information
- Originated from the Latin phrase *minuscula littera* meaning "somewhat small letter."
- **Minuscule** is often misspelled as **miniscule**.

missionary: [MISH-uh-ner-ee] Noun/Adjective
A person sent by a church into an area to carry on evangelism or other activities. (n.)
Pertaining to or connected with religious missions. (adj.)

- The **missionary** visited different communities in the area. (n.)
- The **missionary** work is very challenging but fulfilling. (adj.)

Synonym: clergy, evangelist, messenger, pastor, preacher
Antonym: none
Further Information
- Originated from the Latin word *missio* meaning "act of sending."
- A **missionary** is not necessarily a member of the clergy.

mitigate: [MIT-i-geyt] Verb
To lessen in force or intensity, as wrath, grief, harshness, or pain.
To make less severe.

- There's no way to **mitigate** the errors made last week.
- The team set up processes to **mitigate** possible emergencies.

Synonym: check, diminish, lighten, allay, alleviate
Antonym: aggravate, agitate, extend, increase
Further Information
- Originated from the Latin word *mitis* meaning "mild."
- **Mitigate** implies "lessening harm" while **alleviate** means "to make easier to endure."

mollify: [MOL-uh-fahy] Verb
To soften in feeling or temper, as a person.

- A nice hot tea helps me **mollify** during stressful days.
- Talking calmly can **mollify** an overexcited child when they're upset.

Synonym: pacify, allay, soothe, alleviate, ameliorate
Antonym: aggravate, agitate, excite, incite
Further Information
- Originated from the Latin word *mollis* meaning "soft."
- **Mollify** is to "help soften a temper" while **pacify** means "to restore peace."

momentous: [moh-MEN-tuh s] Adjective
Of great or far-reaching importance or consequence.

- His graduation day is a **momentous** one for him after years of difficult study.
- When the climbers finally reached the peak after many failed attempts, it was a **momentous** moment.

Synonym: important, consequential, crucial, decisive
Antonym: inconsequential, insignificant, meaningless
Further Information
- Originated from the mid-14th century word *moment + ous* meaning "brief portion of time" + a suffix for adjectives.
- **Momentous** evoke stronger emotions than **important**.

REVIEW EXERCISE 26

Match the word with its synonym.

___	1.	maltreat	a.	detailed
___	2.	marquee	b.	pacify
___	3.	memorandum	c.	small
___	4.	merciless	d.	heartless
___	5.	meritorious	e.	crucial
___	6.	meticulous	f.	commendable
___	7.	mews	g.	abuse
___	8.	minuscule	h.	clergy
___	9.	missionary	i.	alley
___	10.	mitigate	j.	diminish
___	11.	mollify	k.	canopy
___	12.	momentous	l.	announcement

From the words above, fill in the blanks with the most appropriate word. The word form may need changing.

1. I lost the _____ puzzle piece under the table.

2. Walking on the moon is a _____ human achievement.

3. The _____ in front of the movie theater shows the movie schedule.

4. Farah being one of the _____students, received an award at the school's annual day.

5. We live in a historical _____ that was renovated years ago.

6. You should never _____ your pets as it is illegal.

7. The panicking crowd was _____ by the host to help them calm down.

8. Advance information about natural disasters may help us _____ their impact.

9. _____ often visit far off countries for their work.

10. The _____ general won the battle with his brutal techniques.

11. The two countries signed a _____ of understanding to promote commerce.

12. The artist is _____ in creating his masterpieces from wood.

WORD SET 27

monotonous: [muh-NOT-n-uh s] Adjective
Lacking in variety; tediously unvarying.
A sound, continuing in one note.

- Sometimes, Sundays are quite **monotonous** when you have nothing planned.
- His **monotonous** tone does not betray any emotion.

Synonym: boring, dreary, dull, humdrum, plodding
Antonym: bright, clear, eventful, exciting, interesting
Further Information
- Originated from the Greek word *monos + tonos* meaning "single or alone" + "tone."
- **Monotonic** is a similar word and means "speaking in an unchanged tone or pitch."

monument: [MON-yuh-muh nt] Noun/Verb
Something erected in memory of a person, event, etc., such as a building, pillar, or statue. (n.)
To build a monument or monuments to; commemorate. (v.)

- The **monument** is being restored and soon will be open to the public. (n.)
- This important event should be **monumented** for future generations. (v.)

Synonym: memorial, remembrance, headstone, pillar, shrine
Antonym: none
Further Information
- Originated from the Latin word *monere* meaning "remind."
- **Monument** implies "efforts to preserve memory."

motivate: [MOH-tuh-veyt] Verb
To provide with a motive, or a cause or reason to act.

- It is imperative for a leader to **motivate** his/her followers.
- Shane always tries to **motivate** himself even during difficult times.

Synonym: stimulate, instigate, drive, excite, persuade
Antonym: discourage, dissuade, halt, hinder
Further Information
- Originated from the Old French word *motif + ate* meaning "moving" + verbal suffix.
- **Motivate** means "to find reason for action" whereas **inspire** means "to arouse positive feeling."

moult: [mohlt] Verb/Noun
(Of birds, insects, reptiles, etc.) To cast or shed the feathers, skin, or the like, that will be replaced by a new growth. (v.)
An act, process, or an instance of moulting/Something that is dropped in moulting. (n.)

- It is normal for some animals to look sickly while **moulting**. (v.)
- The mountain goat is brilliant white after the autumn **moult**. (n.)

Synonym: shed
Antonym: none
Further Information
- Originated from the Latin word *mutare* meaning "to change."
- **Moult** is also spelled as **molt.**

mound: [mound] Noun/Verb
A natural elevation of earth. (n.)
To form into a mound. (v.)

- You can see the river when you stand over that **mound**. (n.)
- The soldiers will **mound** the eastern part of the camp to protect against enemies. (v.)

Synonym: heap, hill, anthill, dune, embankment
Antonym: depression, ditch
Further Information
- Originated from the Middle Dutch word *mond* meaning "protection."
- M**ound** up the rice on a serving plate.

muffled: [MUHF-uh ld] Verb
To wrap with something to deaden or prevent sound.

- The walls are **muffled** for the privacy of the tenants.
- It is important for the ears to be **muffled** when working in a noisy environment.

Synonym: faint, quietened, suppressed, muted
Antonym: loud, audible
Further Information
- Originated from the Old French word *moufle* meaning "thick glove."
- A **muffler** is a part of a vehicle's exhaust system meant to reduce its noise.

mundane: [muhn-DEYN] Adjective
Lacking excitement or interest; Of or relating to this world or earth as contrasted with heaven.

- Sometimes, **mundane** tasks are quite boring and repetitive.
- On weekends, Jeanie likes to have **mundane** moments to relax and let her mind rest.

Synonym: ordinary, banal, day-to-day, every day, humdrum
Antonym: abnormal, uncommon, unusual
Further Information
- Originated from the Latin word *mundus* meaning "world."
- **Mundane** implies "unremarkable."

naval: [ney-vuh l] Adjective
Of or relating to ships of all kinds.
Belonging to, pertaining to, or connected with a navy.

- He is set to study **naval** engineering because he likes to work in ships.
- **Naval** affairs are almost always confidential as required by the government.

Synonym: marine, maritime, seafaring
Antonym: none
Further Information
- Originated from the Latin word *navis* meaning "ship."
- Should not be confused with **navel** which is a part of the human body.

navel: [NEY-vuh l] Noun
A rounded, knotty depression in the center of a person's belly caused by the detachment of the umbilical cord after birth.
The central point or middle of anything or place.

- The umbilical cord is cut right at the **navel** when a baby is born.
- An art museum is being constructed at the **navel** of the city.

Synonym: umbilical, belly-button
Antonym: none
Further Information
- Evolved from several sources such as Sanskrit *nabhila*, Prussian *nabis*, and Greek *omphalos*.
- Should not be confused with **naval** which is "anything related to sea-faring or ships."

nebulous: [NEB-yuh-luh s] Adjective
Hazy, vague, indistinct, or confused.

- Jimmy was so sleepy he had only a **nebulous** memory of the meeting.
- A star cluster with large amount of gases is quite **nebulous**.

Synonym: confused, cloudy, ambiguous, murky, hazy
Antonym: bright, certain, clear, definite
Further Information
- Originated from the Latin word *nebula* meaning "mist."
- A related term, **amorphous**, means "lacking definite form."

necessity: [nuh-SES-i-tee] Noun
Something necessary or indispensable.
An essential requirement or need for something.

- It is a **necessity** to review your homework before submitting it.
- Jim packed all the **necessities** for the trip.

Synonym: essential, fundamental, obligation, precondition, requirement
Antonym: auxiliary, extra, trivia
Further Information
- Originated from the Latin *necesse* meaning "needful."
- **Necessity** implies "being required or needed" while **unavoidability** implies "something that will happen."

negate: [ni-GEYT] Verb
To deny the existence, evidence, or truth of.
To nullify or cause to be ineffective.

- The current result of the experiment **negates** the earlier hypothesis.
- The efforts of the team are **negated** by the lack of funds.

Synonym: contradict, annihilate, belie, cancel, disallow
Antonym: allow, approve, do
Further Information
- Originated from the Latin word *negatio* meaning "denial."
- **Negate** means "to deny the existence" while **negative** is "the opposite of/not desirable."

REVIEW EXERCISE 27

Match the word with its synonym.

___	1.	monotonous	a.	banal
___	2.	monument	b.	umbilical
___	3.	motivate	c.	cloudy
___	4.	moult	d.	marine
___	5.	mound	e.	dreary
___	6.	muffled	f.	memorial
___	7.	mundane	g.	shed
___	8.	naval	h.	contradict
___	9.	navel	i.	stimulate
___	10.	nebulous	j.	essential
___	11.	necessity	k.	hill
___	12.	negate	l.	muted

From the words above, fill in the blanks with the most appropriate word. The word form may need changing.

1. In some cultures, a baby's _____ is usually covered to protect from infection.

2. Some teachers are very good at _____ their students.

3. I am padding the walls so that the noise is _____ and I won't be disturbed at night.

4. Being active is a _____ for a healthy life.

5. Boring summers can be _____ when you are not on vacation somewhere.

6. Historical figures are commemorated with _____ and landmarks.

7. Snakes _____ to replace their old skins.

8. Some fish species like the Goldfish are known to have _____ memories.

9. The _____ officer is a veteran captain of the ship.

10. Life can be _____ with short adventures in between.

11. We flattened the _____ to make way for the garden.

12. His bad attitude _____ his efforts and achievements.

WORD SET 28

nonsensical: [non-SEN-si-kuh l] Adjective
(Of words or language) Having little or no meaning.
(Of behavior, conduct, actions, etc.) Foolish, senseless, fatuous, or absurd.

- The **nonsensical** words of the baby are quite adorable.
- He is difficult to understand because of his **nonsensical** attitude.

Synonym: absurd, ridiculous, senseless, silly, stupid
Antonym: intelligent, reasonable, sensible, serious
Further Information
- Originated from *non + sense + ical* meaning "lack of" + "perception" + adjectival suffix.
- **Nonsensical** and **senseless** are interchangeable.

notorious: [noh-TAWR-ee-uh s] Adjective
Widely and unfavorably known.
Publicly or generally known, typically for some bad quality or deed.

- Karl is **notorious** for being a latecomer.
- Celebrities are **notorious** for their sensationalism.

Synonym: infamous, egregious, outrageous, notable, renowned
Antonym: inconspicuous, unknown
Further Information
- Originated from the Latin word *notus* meaning "known."
- **Notorious** connotes "being known for something unfavorable."

novice: [NOV-is] Noun
A person who is new to the circumstances, work, etc., in which he or she is placed.

- **Novice** workers are often trained by senior managers.
- Every year, **novice** members of the clergy are introduced to the church.

Synonym: beginner, learner, neophyte, newcomer
Antonym: expert, professional
Further Information
- Originated from the Late Latin word *novus* meaning "new."
- In religions, a **novice** is "a person who has been received into a religious order or congregation for a period of probation."

nurture: [NUR-cher] Verb/Noun
To feed and protect. (v.)
Rearing, upbringing, training, education, or the like. (n.)

- Mothers typically have the natural instinct to **nurture**. (v.)
- The **nurture** of young scientists is very important. (n.)

Synonym: development, breeding, care, nourishment
Antonym: ignorance, neglect, negligence
<u>Further Information</u>
- Originated from the Latin word *nutrire* meaning "feed or cherish."
- In Biology, **nurture** means "the environmental factors that partly determine the structure of an organism."

oasis: [oh-EY-sis] Noun
A small fertile or green area in a desert region, usually having a spring or well.
Something serving as a refuge, relief, or pleasant change from what is usual, annoying, difficult, etc.

- It is difficult to find an **oasis** in the very hot desert.
- The library is a valuable **oasis** in an otherwise busy city.

Synonym: spring, fountain, well, haven, sanctuary
Antonym: none
<u>Further Information</u>
- Virtually unchanged from its Late Latin form *oasis* meaning "dwelling place."
- **Oasis** implies "a place of refuge in a harsh environment."

obese: [oh-BEES] Adjective
Very fat or overweight.

- The doctor warned him to avoid eating too much or else he will become **obese**.
- That fat cat is too fluffy and **obese** to be healthy.

Synonym: overweight, corpulent
Antonym: skinny, underweight
<u>Further Information</u>
- Originated from the Latin word *edere* meaning "eat."
- **Obese** is relatively heavier than **overweight**.

obligatory: [ob-li-guh-TAWR-ee] Adjective
Required as a matter of legal, moral or other rule.

- A lengthy speech is desirable but not **obligatory**.
- You have to do the **obligatory** interview of the visiting alumni.

Synonym: essential, compulsory, imperative, mandatory, requisite
Antonym: free, optional, unnecessary
Further Information
- Originated from the Late Latin word *obligatorius* meaning "binding."
- The synonym **compulsory** is generally used in contexts of education and business while **obligatory** refers to laws and rules.

oblige: [uh-BLAHYJ] Verb
To require or constrain, as by law, command, conscience, or force of necessity.
To place under a debt of gratitude for some benefit, favor, or service.

- Once signed, you are **obliged** to follow the contract.
- I'm **obliged** to you for the help you have provided.

Synonym: require, bind, compel, gratify, please
Antonym: release, frustrate, upset
Further Information
- Originated from the Latin word *ob + ligare* meaning "toward" + "to bind."
- In Law, **oblige** is "to bind by a verbal agreement or a contract."
- Obligatory is the adjectival form of oblige.

oblivious: [uh-BLIV-ee-uh s] Adjective
Unmindful or unconscious.
Without remembrance or memory.

- Sam becomes **oblivious** to his surroundings when reading books.
- The campers were clearly **oblivious** to the danger.

Synonym: unaware, ignorant, blind, inattentive, uninformed
Antonym: attentive, aware
Further Information
- Originated from the Old Latin word *ob + levis* meaning "over" + "smooth."
- Should not be confused with **obvious** which means "easily seen or recognized."
- Usually followed by **of** or **to**.

obnoxious: [uh b-NOK-shuh s] Adjective
Highly objectionable or offensive.
Annoying or objectionable due to being a show off or attracting undue attention to oneself.

- They did not like his **obnoxious** behavior.
- Smith was quite **obnoxious** and loud during the party.

Synonym: offensive, repulsive, abhorrent, annoying, disgusting
Antonym: agreeable, decent, friendly, good
Further Information
- Originated from the Latin word *ob + noxa* meaning "toward" + "harm."
- **Obnoxious** evoke a stronger negative connotation than **unpleasant** or **annoying**.

obstinate: [OB-stuh-nit] Adjective
Firmly or stubbornly adhering to one's purpose, opinion, etc.
Not easily controlled or overcome.

- He had an **obstinate** determination to pursue a career in films.
- The **obstinate** problem of unemployment has dogged every government.

Synonym: stubborn, adamant, dogmatic, inflexible, steadfast
Antonym: amenable, flexible, obedient, pliant, soft
Further Information
- Originated from the Latin word *ob + stinare* meaning "by" + "to stand or be firm."
- **Obstinate** implies "strong belief in one's ideas" while **obdurate** implies "being unconvinced by others."

obtrusive: [uh b-TROO-siv] Adjective
Noticeable or prominent in an unwelcome way.

- The **obtrusive** child kept yelling during the movie.
- Dad removed the **obtrusive** branch outside the window.

Synonym: pushy, obvious, noticeable, meddlesome
Antonym: modest, shy, unnoticeable
Further Information
- Originated from the Latin word *ob + trudere + ive* meaning "in front of" + "to thrust" + adjectival suffix.
- **Obtrusive** is "to be noticeable in an unwelcome way" while **intrusive** means "to interfere in an annoying way."

REVIEW EXERCISE 28

Match the word with its synonym.

___ 1.	nonsensical	a.	overweight
___ 2.	notorious	b.	ignorant
___ 3.	novice	c.	spring
___ 4.	nurture	d.	infamous
___ 5.	oasis	e.	newcomer
___ 6.	obese	f.	require
___ 7.	obligatory	g.	meddlesome
___ 8.	oblige	h.	repulsive
___ 9.	oblivious	i.	compulsory
___ 10.	obnoxious	j.	care
___ 11.	obstinate	k.	senseless
___ 12.	obtrusive	l.	stubborn

From the words above, fill in the blanks with the most appropriate word. The word form may need changing.

1. _____ is a sign of deteriorating diet and lack of exercise.

2. It is difficult to change the mind of an _____ person.

3. Jean was _____ of the storm outside.

4. An _____ is a valuable source of water and vegetation.

5. Sheila can be _____ and loud during parties.

6. A student is _____ to finish all school work before the summer.

7. The _____ carpenter is learning a lot from his mentor.

8. The _____ graduation speech can be long and monotonous.

9. The road construction work is _____ to the daily traffic.

10. Danny's stories are sometimes _____ and silly.

11. The _____ vandal was finally caught by the police.

12. A mother's _____ touch is irreplaceable and highly valuable.

WORD SET 29

occupation: [ok-yuh-PEY-shuh n] Noun
A person's usual or principal work or business, especially as a means of earning a living.
Possession, settlement, or use of land or property.

- People in a full time **occupation** tend to have structured lives.
- The Roman **occupation** of Britain lasted for a long time.

Synonym: profession, job, affair, craft, employment
Antonym: pastime, hobby, entertainment
<u>Further Information</u>
- Originated from the Latin word *occupare* meaning "a taking possession, business or employment."
- **Occupation** implies "an activity done with compensation; a job" while a **profession** implies "a specialization that often requires training and schooling."
- **Avocation** is a related word meaning "minor occupation or hobby."

odious: [oh-dee-uh s] Adjective
Deserving or causing hatred; Highly offensive.

- He had very few friends because of his **odious** and obnoxious attitude.
- Taking the trash out is such an **odious** task that sometimes I don't want to do.

Synonym: hateful, horrible, abhorrent, abominable, disgusting
Antonym: attractive, delightful, good, kind, likeable
<u>Further Information</u>
- Originated from the Latin word *odium* meaning "hatred."
- Should not be confused with **odorous** meaning "having a characteristic smell or odor."

optimal: [OP-tuh-muh l] Adjective
Best or most favorable.

- The **optimal** way to the grocery store is through 12th Street.
- Engineers often think of **optimal** and efficient methods to do things.

Synonym: excellent, fast, flawless, ideal, best
Antonym: none
<u>Further Information</u>
- Originated from the Latin word *optimus + al m*eaning "best" + suffix forming adjective.
- Another form of **optimal** is **optimum**.

orator: [AWR-uh-ter] Noun
A public speaker, especially one of great eloquence.

- Cicero is known to be one of the greatest **orators** of ancient Greece.
- **Orators** usually have natural charm and confidence that captivates the audience.

Synonym: speaker, lecturer
Antonym: none
Further Information
- Originated from the Latin word *orare* meaning "to speak or speak before a court or assembly."
- **Orator** implies "a person who delivers a speech" whereas **narrator** is "a person who gives an account or tells the story of events, experiences, etc."

orchestrate: [AWR-kuh-streyt] Verb
To compose or arrange (music) for performance by an orchestra.
To arrange or manipulate, especially by means of clever or thorough planning or manoeuvring.

- Janis is tasked to **orchestrate** new pieces for the orchestra for the concert next year.
- No one knew who **orchestrated** the attack which damaged the plaza.

Synonym: organize, arrange, coordinate, manage, set up
Antonym: disperse, divide, separate
Further Information
- Originated from the Greek word *orkhestra* referring to the semicircular space for a performance.
- **Orchestrate** implies "creating musical pieces for an orchestra" while **compose** is "a general term for creating pieces of music."

oscillate: [OS-uh-leyt] Verb
To swing or move to and fro.
To move back and forth between differing beliefs, opinions, conditions, etc.

- It is interesting to see the pendulum **oscillate**.
- I **oscillated** between fear and fun during the comedic horror movie.

Synonym: back-and-forth, fluctuate, lurch, teeter, vacillate
Antonym: remain, stay
Further Information
- Originated from the French word *oscillare* meaning "to swing."
- **Oscillate** is the "regular and continuous change from one form to another" while **fluctuate** means the "irregular change in magnitude or direction."

padlock: [PAD-lok] Noun/Verb
A portable or detachable lock with a pivoted or sliding shackle that can be passed through a link, ring, staple, or the like. (n.)
To fasten with or as with a padlock. (v.)

- He bought a stronger **padlock** for his house because of the break-ins around the area. (n.)
- Please **padlock** the store after you leave, as you left it open last time. (v.)

Synonym: bolt, fastener, latch, blockade, closure
Antonym: none
Further Information
- Originated from the late 15th century word *pad + lock* meaning "to fasten or secure."
- A **padlock** is "something portable that is used to secure something" while a **lock** is "a general term for a locking device typically built-in."

palatial: [puh-LEY-shuh l] Adjective
Of, relating to, or resembling a palace.
Befitting or suitable for a palace.

- Sandra's house is quite **palatial** with 10 rooms and 6 bathrooms.
- This figurine is so beautiful; it is **palatial** and elegant.

Synonym: grand, opulent, deluxe, imposing, luxurious
Antonym: common, poor, unimpressive
Further Information
- Originated from the Latin word *palatium* referring to the Palatine Hill.
- Should not be confused with the word **palatable** meaning "acceptable or agreeable to the taste."

parched: [pahrch d] Verb
To make extremely, excessively, or completely dry, as heat, sun, and wind do.
To suffer from heat, thirst, or need of water.

- Failure of rains caused the land to become **parched**.
- The runners crossed the finish line with parched throats, gasping for breath.

Synonym: dry, arid, scorched, thirsty, withered
Antonym: moist, wet
Further Information
- Originated from the Latin word *persiccare* meaning "to dry thoroughly."
- **Parched** refers to smaller items or wanting water while **arid** refers to the weather or to a large area.

parry: [PAR-ee] Verb/Noun
To ward off (a thrust, stroke, weapon, etc.). (v.)
An act or instance of parrying. (n.)

- They **parried** with difficult questions during the debate. (v.)
- The knights' swords clashed in a **parry**. (n.)

Synonym: anticipate, avoid, block, bypass, deflect
Antonym: allow, attract
Further Information
- Originated from the Italian word *parare* meaning "ward off."
- **Parry** is "to avoid" while **block** is "to obstruct."

partisan: [pahr-tuh-ZAN] Noun/Adjective
An adherent or supporter of a person, group, party, or cause, especially a person who shows a biased, emotional allegiance. (n.)
Of, relating to, or characteristic of partisans; partial to a specific party, person, etc. (adj.)

- The political party **partisans** claimed that the TV news was biased against them. (n.)
- Newspapers have become increasingly **partisan**. (adj.)

Synonym: interested, factional, biased, one-sided, sectarian
Antonym: fair, unbiased
Further Information
- Originated from the Italian word *parte* meaning "part."
- A **partisan** implies "being a member of a certain group" while a **follower** is "someone who follows a certain directive."

peculiar: [pi-KYOOL-yer] Adjective/Noun
Distinctive in nature or character from others. (adj.)
An exclusive property or privilege belonging to a person. (n.)

- The **peculiar** painting combines many colors in one piece of work. (adj.)
- He is considered a **peculiar** because of his obsession with costumes. (n.)

Synonym: characteristic, distinguishing, distinct, particular, strange, unique
Antonym: common, general, indefinite, like, normal
Further Information
- Originated from the Latin word *pecu* meaning "cattle."
- **Peculiar** implies "unique or one-of-a-kind" while **odd** means "different from the general public."

REVIEW EXERCISE 29

Match the word with its synonym.

___	1.	occupation	a.	bolt
___	2.	odious	b.	block
___	3.	optimal	c.	biased
___	4.	orator	d.	opulent
___	5.	orchestrate	e.	manage
___	6.	oscillate	f.	speaker
___	7.	padlock	g.	unique
___	8.	palatial	h.	fluctuate
___	9.	parched	i.	job
___	10.	parry	j.	ideal
___	11.	partisan	k.	dry
___	12.	peculiar	l.	horrible

From the words above, fill in the blanks with the most appropriate word. The word form may need changing.

1. One's _____ is ideally his expertise and interest.

2. We need to use a bigger _____ for the door for added security.

3. I'm _____ after an intense workout using weights and machines.

4. Impactful_____ are typically charming and full of personality.

5. Kings and queens own _____ properties around the country.

6. Swings _____ back and forth, which makes them very popular with kids.

7. The _____ TV host favored one side of the debate.

8. _____ processes can save time and effort and make workers more productive.

9. The _____ remark received condemnation from everyone.

10. Jimmy _____ the whole project right up to its successful conclusion.

11. His butterfly and moth collection is quite _____.

12. Swordsmen _____ with one another to practice their skills.

WORD SET 30

pendant: [PEN-duh nt] Noun
A hanging ornament, such as an earring or the main piece suspended from a necklace.
That by which something is suspended, as the ringed stem of a watch.

- Her grandmother gave her a **pendant** as a birthday gift.
- The diamond **pendant** costs quite a lot compared to the other pieces of jewelry.

Synonym: beads, choker, necklace, rosary
Antonym: none
<u>Further Information</u>
- Originated from the Latin word *pendere* meaning "to hang."
- Should not be confused with the adjective **pendent** meaning "hanging down."

pensive: [PEN-siv] Adjective
Dreamily or wistfully thoughtful.
Expressing or revealing thoughtfulness, usually marked by some sadness.

- Kevin likes to spend time under the apple trees when he is in a **pensive** mood.
- The **pensive** song impressed everyone in the concert with its thoughtful lyrics.

Synonym: meditative, solemn, contemplative, dreamy, sober
Antonym: negligent, uncaring
<u>Further Information</u>
- Originated from the Latin word *pensare* meaning "weigh or consider."
- Should not be confused with the word **pensieve** which is a fictional object from the book series *Harry Potter*.

perception: [per-SEP-shuh n] Noun
The act or faculty of perceiving, or apprehending by means of the senses or of the mind.
Immediate or intuitive recognition or appreciation, as of moral, psychological, or aesthetic qualities.

- Their **perception** of the current policies made them reject the idea.
- He has a unique **perception** when it comes to painting and the visual arts.

Synonym: understanding, idea, approach, attention, attitude
Antonym: concrete, ignorance, stupidity
<u>Further Information</u>
- Originated from the Latin word *percipere* meaning "seize or understand."
- Should not be confused with **perspective** which means "view point."

perceptive: [per-SEP-tiv] Adjective
Having or showing keenness of insight, understanding, or intuition.

- Amanda is quite a **perceptive** child, as she notices a lot of things around her.
- Problems need **perceptive** answers to fully solve the root cause.

Synonym: alert, sensitive, astute, discerning, discreet
Antonym: careless, foolish, idiotic, ignorant, stupid
Further Information
- Originated from the Anglo-French word *parceif + ive* meaning "to notice or see" + adjective forming suffix.
- Should not be confused with **receptive** meaning "having the quality of receiving or taking."

peripheral: [puh-RIF-er-uh l] Adjective
Concerned with relatively minor, irrelevant, or superficial aspects of the subject in question.
Pertaining to, situated in, or constituting the edge.

- During meetings, we should avoid talking about **peripheral** issues too much.
- The Jackson family lives in the **peripheral** part of the town.

Synonym: minor, outer, outside, incidental, tangential
Antonym: central
Further Information
- Evolved from the Greek words *peri* which means "around" and *pherein* which means "to bear" and *al* which is a suffix with the general sense "of the kind of."
- In Anatomy, **peripheral** means "near the surface or outside of."
- Other words having the same prefix **peri** are perimeter, periscope, perigee etc.

permeate: [PUR-mee-eyt] Verb
To pass into or through every part of.
To spread throughout something.

- The smell of freshly baked cookies **permeated** the entire house.
- Acids usually **permeate** most metallic surfaces.

Synonym: filter, imbue, impregnate, infiltrate, infuse
Antonym: dehydrate, dry, take out
Further Information
- Originated from the Latin word *per + meare* meaning "through" + "pass or go."
- **Permeate** is "to pass through" while **penetrate** implies "to break through."

perpetuate: [per-PECH-oo-eyt] Verb
To cause to continue or prevail indefinitely.

- Naming the library after its founder **perpetuates** his memory.
- It might be best to back off and not **perpetuate** the argument.

Synonym: bolster, maintain, preserve
Antonym: discontinue, give up, halt
Further Information
- Originated from the Latin word *perpetuus* meaning "continuing throughout."
- Should not be confused with **perpetrate** meaning "to commit/to carry out."

pervasive: [per-VEY-siv] Adjective
(Especially of an unwelcome influence or physical effect) Spreading widely throughout an area or a group of people.

- The epidemic is alarming the authorities as it becomes **pervasive**.
- Ageism is **pervasive** and entrenched in our society.

Synonym: extensive, common, inescapable, omnipresent, prevalent
Antonym: rare, scarce
Further Information
- Originated from the Latin word *pervadere + ive* meaning "to spread" + adjective forming suffix.
- Should not be confused with **persuasive** meaning "having the power or ability to persuade."

petty: [PET-ee] Adjective
Of little or no importance or consequence.
Of lesser or secondary importance, merit, etc.

- **Petty** arguments are often a waste of time and effort.
- No one likes a **petty** person who creates unnecessary tension in the group.

Synonym: trivial, insignificant, frivolous, lesser, minor
Antonym: greater, major
Further Information
- Originated from the French word *petit* meaning "small."
- Should not be confused with **pretty** meaning "pleasing or attractive to the eye."

philanthropy: [fi-LAN-thruh-pee] Noun
Selfless concern for human welfare and advancement.
The activity of donating to such persons or purposes in this way.

- Many hospitals were built as a result of private **philanthropy.**
- We are teaching our child the value of **philanthropy**, as it promotes kindness and empathy.

Synonym: humanitarianism, charity, generosity
Antonym: *none*
Further Information
- Originated from the Greek word *phil + anthropos* meaning "loving" + "mankind."
- **Philanthropy** implies "long term, strategic giving, focused on re-building" while **charity** refers to "short term immediate response, focused on rescue and relief."

pinnacle: [PIN-uh-kuh l] Noun
The highest or culminating point, as of success, power, fame, etc.
To place on or as on a pinnacle.

- Receiving the award is the **pinnacle** of his career because of his dedication and efforts.
- The brothers have reached the **pinnacle** of sport.

Synonym: top, crest, apex, culmination, greatest
Antonym: bottom, nadir
Further Information
- Originated from the Late Latin word *pinna* meaning "wing or point."
- **Pinnacle** evokes a stronger emotion than **peak**.

pious: [PAHY-uh s] Adjective
Having or showing a dutiful spirit of reverence for God or an earnest wish to fulfil religious obligations.
(Of a hope) Sincere but unlikely to be fulfilled.

- Saints are **pious** and devoted to their beliefs even to the point of sacrificing their lives.
- The **pious** literature contains historical accounts of the religion.

Synonym: dedicated, religious, devout, righteous
Antonym: impious, irreligious
Further Information
- Originated from the Latin word *pius* + ous meaning "dutiful" + adjective suffix.
- **Pious** implies "devotion to a belief or religion."

REVIEW EXERCISE 30

Match the word with its synonym.

___	1.	pendant	a.	understanding
___	2.	pensive	b.	solemn
___	3.	perception	c.	astute
___	4.	perceptive	d.	outer
___	5.	peripheral	e.	infiltrate
___	6.	permeate	f.	devout
___	7.	perpetuate	g.	necklace
___	8.	pervasive	h.	charity
___	9.	petty	i.	extensive
___	10.	philanthropy	j.	trivial
___	11.	pinnacle	k.	apex
___	12.	pious	l.	maintain

From the words above, fill in the blanks with the most appropriate word. The word form may need changing.

1.   Doing nothing will only _____ the problem.

2.   The whole house was _____ by the smell of the burned cookies.

3.   The _____ student understood the topic of the discussion right away.

4.   Minny's _____ vision was damaged by the accident.

5.   I am sometimes overcome by a _____ mood during winter.

6.   Some animals are known to be _____ species that can destroy an ecosystem.

7.   His _____ of the problem is quite accurate and to the point.

8.   His _____ devotion is recognised by the Church and the society.

9.   _____ changes the lives of people who have no hope.

10.   The silver _____ was designed by a famous jeweller.

11.   _____ theft is stealing an item of low value.

12.   Winning the award is the _____ of his career in real estate.

WORD SET 31

pique: [peek] Verb/Noun
To arouse an emotion or provoke to action. (v.)
A feeling of irritation or resentment, as from a wound to pride or self-esteem. (n.)

- His interest was **piqued** when he saw the discount. (v.)
- Johnson was in a **pique** when he was not invited to the party. (n.)

Synonym: anger, irritation, annoy, arouse, displease
Antonym: delight, happiness, pleasure
<u>Further Information</u>
- Originated from the French word *piquer* meaning "to prick or sting."
- Also pronounced **piqué** [pi-KEY] meaning "a fabric of cotton, spun rayon, or silk, woven lengthwise with raised cords.

pivotal: [PIV-uh-tl] Adjective
Of, relating to, or serving as a pivot.
Of vital or critical importance.

- The **pivotal** character in the movie was not very convincing.
- Being promoted was a **pivotal** moment of his career in software development.

Synonym: important, central, climactic, critical, crucial
Antonym: inessential, minor, secondary, trivial, uncritical
<u>Further Information</u>
- Originated from the French word *pue* which means "tooth of a comb" and the Spanish word *puya* which means "point."
- **Pivotal** implies "a moment which caused significant change."

placate: [PLEY-keyt] Verb
To appease or pacify, especially by concessions or conciliatory gestures.

- The CEO tried to **placate** the angry directors during the board meeting.
- The mother used a stuffed toy to **placate** the crying baby.

Synonym: soothe, pacify, appease, assuage, mollify
Antonym: agitate, incite, irritate, provoke, upset
<u>Further Information</u>
- Originated from the Latin word *placere* meaning "to please."
- Should not be confused with **placard** which means "a paperboard sign or notice, as one posted in a public place or carried by a demonstrator or picketer."

platonic: [pluh-TON-ik] Adjective
Of, relating to, or characteristic of the Greek philosopher Plato or his doctrines.
Free from sensual desire, especially in a relationship between two persons of the opposite sex.

- A lot of his students challenged the **Platonic** philosophy.
- Friends typically have **platonic** relationships that are built over time.

Synonym: transcendent, utopian, chaste
Antonym: physical
Further Information
- Originated from the Greek word *Platonikos* referring to the followers of Plato.
- Should not be confused with **plutonic** which refers to a class of igneous rocks.

pliable: [PLAHY-uh-buh l] Adjective
Easily bent or flexible.
Easily influenced or persuaded.

- Leather is usually dried under the sun to make it **pliable**.
- Teachers shape the **pliable** minds of children to help them grow into effective adults.

Synonym: bendable, adaptable, docile, flexible, limber, yielding
Antonym: hard, inflexible, obstinate, rigid, stiff
Further Information
- Originated from the French word *plier + ply* meaning "to bend" + adjectival suffix.
- **Pliable** implies "ability to change shape" while **malleable** means "capable of being extended."

pliers: [PLAHY-er s] Noun
Small pincers with long jaws, for bending wire, holding small objects, etc.

- **Pliers** are used to grip and tighten objects, especially nuts and bolts.
- Can you buy the high-end **pliers** at the store?

Synonym: pincers, forceps, tongs
Antonym: none
Further Information
- Originated from the Latin word *plicare* meaning "to fold."
- **Pliers** can also be spelled as **plyers** (British).

podcast: [POD-kast] Noun/Verb
A digital audio or video file or recording, usually part of a themed series, that can be downloaded from a website to a media player or computer. (n.)
To record and upload as a podcast. (v.)

- I love listening to **podcasts** about music and artists. (n.)
- We are scheduled to **podcast** tomorrow night during primetime. (v.)

Synonym: recording
Antonym: none
Further Information
- Combination of 21st century words *iPod + broadcast*.
- **Podcast** typically refers to recorded discussions about topics.

populous: [POP-yuh-luh s] Adjective
Full of residents or inhabitants, such as a region.
Jammed or crowded with people.

- The **populous** city is becoming industrialized because new companies are flocking to it.
- Shanghai is one of the most **populous** cities in the world.

Synonym: crowded, numerous, populated, various
Antonym: deserted
Further Information
- Originated from the Late Latin word *populus* meaning "people."
- **Populous** refers to the number of people in an area while **populace** refers to the inhabitants of a place.

pore: [pohr] Verb/Noun
To read or study with steady attention or application. (v.)
A small opening or orifice, as in the skin or a leaf, for perspiration, absorption, etc. (n.)

- The students **pored** over the old statue at the museum. (v.)
- Sweat poured from every **pore** in the runner's body. (n.)

Synonym: brood, contemplate, look, examine, muse
Antonym: disregard, ignore, forget
Further Information
- Originated from the Greek word *poros* meaning "pore or passage."

postpone: [pohst-POHN] Verb
To put off to a later time.
To place after in order of importance or estimation.

- Smith had to **postpone** the meeting because they were all busy.
- He had to **postpone** his dream of becoming an artist.

Synonym: adjourn, defer, delay, shelve, suspend
Antonym: advance, continue, expedite, forward, further
Further Information
- Originated from the Latin word *post + ponere* meaning "after" + "to place."
- **Postpone** is "to do something at a later time" while **defer** means "to decide something later on."

poverty: [POV-er-tee] Noun
The state or condition of having little or no money, goods, or means of support.
Deficiency of necessary or desirable ingredients, qualities, etc.

- There is rampant **poverty** in some parts of the city.
- The **poverty** of the soil makes it unfit for crops.

Synonym: lack, deficit, famine, scarcity, shortage, underdevelopment
Antonym: abundance, ease, enough, excess, plenty
Further Information
- Originated from the Latin word *pauper* meaning "poor."
- **Poverty** implies "lack of necessities" while **destitution** implies "a state of having absolutely none of the necessities."

preamble: [PREE-am-buh l] Noun
An introductory statement.
The introductory part of a statute, deed, or the like, stating the reasons and intent of what follows.

- He opened the program with a quick **preamble** about the history of the town.
- A **preamble** was written by the author for his new book.

Synonym: opening, beginning, foreword, prologue, prelude
Antonym: epilogue, appendix, conclusion, afterword, closing
Further Information
- Originated from the Late Latin word *praeambulus* meaning "going before."
- A **preamble** also refers to the introductory statement in a constitution.

REVIEW EXERCISE 31

Match the word with its synonym.

___	1.	pique	a.	pacify
___	2.	pivotal	b.	delay
___	3.	placate	c.	lack
___	4.	platonic	d.	pincers
___	5.	pliable	e.	important
___	6.	pliers	f.	beginning
___	7.	podcast	g.	arouse
___	8.	populous	h.	chaste
___	9.	pore	i.	yielding
___	10.	postpone	j.	examine
___	11.	poverty	k.	recording
___	12.	preamble	l.	crowded

From the words above, fill in the blanks with the most appropriate word. The word form may need changing.

1. _____ is a global problem that is still plaguing many countries.

2. I like downloading _____ on my phone and listening to them on my commute.

3. The _____ in my toolbox are missing so I went to the hardware store to get a new pair.

4. The movie trailer_____ my interest, so I went to the cinema to watch the movie.

5. Their _____ relationship grew stronger after years of ups and downs.

6. The book's _____ revealed the author's inspiration for writing the book.

7. I _____ over the classified ads for open positions in big companies, because I

   was looking for a job change.

8. The _____ role in the movie was given to the new actor.

9. The area is becoming more _____ as more businesses are created.

10. _____ the boss when he gets angry and avoid being angry as well.

11. Clay is perfect for sculpting as it is _____.

12. The concert was _____ because of the storm.

WORD SET 32

predicament: [pri-DIK-uh-muh nt] Noun
An unpleasantly difficult, perplexing, or dangerous situation.

- Jane needs all the help she can get to overcome her **predicament**.
- Careless decisions can get you in a **predicament**.

Synonym: circumstance, crisis, deadlock, dilemma, hardship
Antonym: advantage, agreement, benefit, blessing, breakthrough
<u>Further Information</u>
- Originated from the Latin word *prae + dicare* meaning "forth or before" + "proclaim."
- **Predicament** refers to "generally negative situation" while **dilemma** refers to "puzzling situation."

preliminary: [pri-LIM-uh-ner-ee] Adjective/Noun
Preceding and leading up to the main part, matter, or business. (adj.)
Something that is an introductory or preparatory step, measure, contest, etc. (n.)

- A **preliminary** discussion was conducted to prepare for the workshop. (adj.)
- He needs to take the **preliminary** exam before the finals. (n.)

Synonym: initial, exploratory, preparatory, prior
Antonym: additional, extra
<u>Further Information</u>
- Originated from the Lati wordn *prae + limen* meaning "before" + "threshold."
- **Preliminary** means "something that comes before the main subject" while **preparatory** is "preparing for the main idea."

prepay: [pree-PEY] Verb
To pay or arrange to pay beforehand or before due.

- Banks usually allow you to **prepay** your loan.
- **Prepaying** allows for better management of one's finances.

Synonym: pay, compensate, disburse, advance
Antonym: deny, deprive, refuse
<u>Further Information</u>
- Originated from the Latin word *pre + pay* meaning "before" + "to settle a debt."
- **Prepay** is "paying before due" while **postpaid** is "to pay after usage."

pretentious: [pri-TEN-shuh s] Adjective
Characterized by assumption of dignity or importance, especially when exaggerated or undeserved.

- A **pretentious** person is not liked by anyone.
- They avoided the **pretentious** businessman and chose someone who was genuine.

Synonym: snobbish, conceited, arty, exaggerated, hollow
Antonym: genuine, honest, moderate, modest, plain
Further Information
- Originated from the Latin word *prae + tendere* meaning "before" + "to claim."
- Should not be confused with **precocious** meaning "unusually advanced or mature in development, especially mental development."

proficient: [pruh-FISH-uh nt] Adjective
Well-advanced or competent in any art, science, or subject.

- Janice is **proficient** in both Maths and Chemistry.
- He was **proficient** at his job and was soon promoted.

Synonym: able, skilled, accomplished, adept
Antonym: ignorant, immature, impotent, incapable, incompetent
Further Information
- Originated from the Latin word *pro + facere* meaning "on behalf of" + "do or make."
- An **expert** is better than someone who is merely **proficient**.

profligate: [PROF-li-geyt] Adjective/Noun
Utterly and shamelessly immoral or dissipated; Recklessly wasteful or extravagant. (adj.)
A profligate person. (n.)

- The **profligate** president spent the company's money on personal expenses. (adj.)
- The heiress is a **profligate** who wants the most expensive things. (n.)

Synonym: immoral, corrupt, depraved, unprincipled, wasteful, extravagant
Antonym: gentle, moral
Further Information
- Originated from the Latin word *pro + fligere* meaning "forward" + "strike down."
- **Profligate** (n.) is someone who "engages in immoral and wasteful acts" while **prodigal** (n.) implies "someone who was immoral but is now reformed, as in the prodigal son who eventually comes back home."

proposal: [pruh-POH-zuh l] Noun
The act of offering or suggesting something for acceptance, adoption, or performance.

- The **proposal** for the science project is quite impressive.
- **Proposals** should always be clear and convincing.

Synonym: suggestion, bid, idea, motion, offer
Antonym: condemnation, refusal
Further Information
- Originated from the Old French word *pro + poser + al* meaning "forth" + "put or place" + adjectival suffix.
- A **proposal** also means "an offer of marriage."

prospective: [pruh-SPEK-tiv] Adjective
Of or in the future.
Potential, likely, or expected.

- He is so excited to send applications to **prospective** colleges.
- Jane is meeting with her **prospective** clients.

Synonym: eventual, expected, proposed, soon-to-be, future, potential
Antonym: agreed, concurred
Further Information
- Originated from the Latin word *pro + specere* meaning "forward" + "look at."
- **Prospective** implies "more likely to happen" whereas **potential** implies "may or may not happen."

prosper: [PROS-per] Verb
To be successful or fortunate, especially in financial aspects.

- To **prosper** in one's career is everybody's dream.
- Samantha **prospered** as an artist though her major in university was Economics.

Synonym: bloom, blossom, catch on, do well, flourish
Antonym: fail, languish, shrink, wither, decline
Further Information
- Originated from the Old Latin word *pro + spes* meaning "for" + "hope."
- **Prosper** implies "to succeed in material or financial aspect" while **succeed** implies "to accomplish what is attempted."

prosperous: [PROS-per-uh s] Adjective
Having or characterized by financial success or good fortune.
Well-to-do or well-off.

- It is difficult to maintain a **prosperous** business during an economic meltdown.
- Janna is happy to have a **prosperous** family that supports her.

Synonym: successful, thriving, affluent, booming, comfortable
Antonym: destitute, failing, impoverished, lacking, needy
Further Information
- Originated from the Old Latin *pro + spes + ous* meaning "for" + "hope" + adjectival suffix for nouns.
- **Prosperous** means "the condition of having a good fortune" while **affluence** means "abundance of financial wealth."

pulverize: [puhl-vuh-rahys] Verb
To reduce to dust or powder, as by pounding or grinding.
To demolish or crush completely.

- Make sure to **pulverize** the dried herbs to bring out the flavors.
- Prepare to **pulverize** the competition tomorrow during the marathon.

Synonym: shatter, destroy, crush
Antonym: construct
Further Information
- Originated from the Late Latin word *pulvis* meaning "dust."
- **Pulverize** is spelled **pulverize** in British English.

pungent: [PUHN-juh nt] Adjective
Sharply affecting the organs of taste or smell, as if by a penetrating power.
Caustic, biting, or sharply expressive.

- We need to find the source of that **pungent** smell and get rid of it.
- Team leaders should avoid **pungent** remarks when criticizing.

Synonym: acid, acrid, aromatic, barbed, biting, sharp
Antonym: bland, blunt, calm, dull, gentle
Further Information
- Originated from the Latin word *pungere* meaning "to prick, pierce, or sting."
- **Pungent** generally refers to smell or taste while **potent** refers "to having strength."

REVIEW EXERCISE 32

Match the word with its synonym.

___ 1. predicament   a. conceited
___ 2. preliminary   b. skilled
___ 3. prepay   c. affluent
___ 4. pretentious   d. shatter
___ 5. proficient   e. disburse
___ 6. profligate   f. initial
___ 7. proposal   g. acrid
___ 8. prospective   h. suggestion
___ 9. prosper   i. potential
___ 10. prosperous   j. crisis
___ 11. pulverize   k. flourish
___ 12. pungent   l. extravagant

From the words above, fill in the blanks with the most appropriate word. The word form may need changing.

1. Hard work and _____ are needed to prosper in life.

2. It is better to _____ a loan ahead of time as you may save on interest costs.

3. The _____ buyers looked at several houses before choosing to buy their first home.

4. The _____ lady likes wearing expensive jewelry to impress other people.

5. In the war, many villages were _____ by the enemy bombs.

6. The _____ result of the laboratory test was positive, but we await final confirmation.

7. The candidate swore to put an end to _____ government spending if he was elected.

8. The _____ smell of burnt garlic bread is unpleasant and dizzying.

9. The Mayor's _____ to increase property tax was strongly opposed by homeowners.

10. The _____ family makes large regular donations to charity.

11. The student is _____ in Physics and Maths which prepares him well for a

    career in science.

12. Kenny is in a difficult financial _____ because he did not pay his bills on time.

WORD SET 33

quaint: [kweynt] Adjective
Having an old-fashioned attractiveness or charm.
Strange, peculiar, or unusual in an interesting, pleasing, or amusing way.

- My family bought the **quaint** old house in the village.
- She has a **quaint** sense of humor which some people don't understand.

Synonym: strange, odd, bizarre, curious, fanciful
Antonym: common, grave, normal, ordinary, reasonable
<u>Further Information</u>
- Originated from the Latin word *cognoscere* meaning "come to know well."
- **Quaint** refers to the emotions and atmosphere being evoked while **picturesque** refers to the visual appeal.

quarantine: [KWOR-uh n-teen] Noun/Verb
A strict isolation imposed to prevent the spread of disease; Enforced detention or isolation. (n.)
To put in or subject to quarantine. (v.)

- Many animals die in **quarantine**. (n.)
- In cases of an epidemic, it is important to **quarantine** those who are infected. (v.)

Synonym: isolation, detention, seclusion, sequester, confine
Antonym: combine, free
<u>Further Information</u>
- Originated from the Italian word *quarantina* meaning "forty days."
- **Quarantine** is "to separate from the rest" while **separate** is "to create space between two or more."

quart: [kwawrt] Noun
A unit of liquid measure of capacity, equal to one fourth of a gallon, or 57.749 cubic inches (0.946 liter) in the U.S. and 69.355 cubic inches (1.136 liters) in Great Britain.
A container holding, or capable of holding, a quart.

- Can you add a **quart** of water to the boiling sauce?
- I don't think a **quart** of juice is enough for me, especially during this hot day.

Synonym: none
Antonym: none
<u>Further Information</u>
- Originated from the Latin word *quattor* meaning "four."
- A **quart** is close to one liter in the metric system.

quilt: [kwilt] Noun/Verb
A bedspread or counterpane, especially a thick one. (n.)
To stitch together (two pieces of cloth and a soft interlining), usually in an ornamental pattern. (v.)

- Grandma sent me a beautiful **quilt** as a present. (n.)
- The blue **quilted** jacket was a work of art. (v.)

Synonym: bedspread, blanket, duvet
Antonym: none
Further Information
- Originated from the Latin word *culcita* meaning "mattress or cushion."
- A **quilt** is typically made up of different patterns or fabrics stitched together.

ransack: [RAN-sak] Verb
To search thoroughly or vigorously (a house, receptacle, etc.)
To search through for plunder.

- We found the house **ransacked** when we got home that night.
- The thieves would **ransack** unguarded buildings.

Synonym: comb, gut, loot, pillage, plunder
Antonym: give, offer, protect, receive, find
Further Information
- Originated from the Old Norse word *rann* meaning "house."
- **Ransack** implies "to search through without regard for order" while **pillage** means "to loot or rob by force, especially during war."

realm: [relm] Noun
A royal domain.
The region, sphere, or domain within which anything occurs, prevails, or dominates.

- The Ottoman Empire's **realm** declined due to failed wars and internal conflict.
- Experts still know nothing about the **realm** of dreams or why we dream.

Synonym: dimension, domain, field, sphere, territory
Antonym: none
Further Information
- Originated from the Latin word *regere* meaning "to rule."
- **Realm** is typically used to describe a royalty's territory.

recapitulate: [ree-kuh-PICH-uh-leyt] Verb
To review by a brief summary, as at the end of a speech or discussion.

- The teacher **recapitulated** the lessons from the entire week.
- The lawyer began to **recapitulate** his arguments with care.

Synonym: recap, rehash, summarize
Antonym: none
Further Information
- Originated from the Late Latin word *re + cap*utulum meaning "again" + "chapter."
- **Recapitulate** means "to summarize" while **reiterate** means "to repeat with the goal of reminding."

reconcile: [REK-uh n-sahyl] Verb
To cause (a person) to accept or be resigned to something not desired.
To win over to friendliness; To settle or harmonize.

- It is necessary to **reconcile** different ideas to create unique solutions.
- The two friends **reconciled** their differences by talking it out.

Synonym: accommodate, appease, assuage, conform, coordinate, harmonize, settle
Antonym: agitate, fight, incite, irritate, mismatch
Further Information
- Originated from the Latin word *re + conciliare* meaning "back" + "bring together."
- **Reconcile** involves two or more parties while **forgive** involves one, e.g. you can forgive someone who is dead.

rectify: [REK-tuh-fahy] Verb
To make, put, or set right.
To put right by adjustment or calculation.

- He called Customer Support to **rectify** the problems in his account.
- The captain called to **rectify** the error in the radar to avoid getting lost.

Synonym: amend, fix, improve, redress, remedy.
Antonym: corrupt, harm, hurt, injure, worsen
Further Information
- Originated from the Latin word *rectus* meaning "right."
- **Rectify** implies "correcting an error."

refrain: [ri-FREYN] Verb
To abstain from an impulse to say or do something.

- He promised to **refrain** from eating junk food every day.
- Karl needs to **refrain** from laughing at people when they make mistakes.

Synonym: abstain, avoid, cease, curb, desist
Antonym: carry on, continue, indulge, use, aid
Further Information
- Originated from the Latin word *re + frenare* meaning "back" + "restrain."
- **Refrain** can also refer to a part of a musical piece.
- Often followed by "from."

refute: [ri-FYOOT] Verb
To prove to be false or erroneous, as an opinion or charge.

- The legal charge was **refuted** by the statement of a witness who saw everything.
- The scientist challenged his peers to **refute** his findings.

Synonym: contradict, discredit, counter, disprove, expose
Antonym: agree, aid, allow, approve, assist
Further Information
- Originated from the Latin word *refutare* meaning "repel or rebut."
- **Refute** implies "to prove wrong by presenting another fact or answer."

regal: [REE-guh l] Adjective
Of or relating to a king.
Befitting or resembling a king.

- After the king died, the **regal** court met to decide who should take over the throne.
- The millionaire looks **regal** in that expensive outfit.

Synonym: royal, kingly, magnificent, majestic
Antonym: common
Further Information
- Originated from the Latin word *rex* meaning "king."
- **Regal** is also a musical instrument which is "a small portable organ, furnished with beating reeds and having two bellows."

REVIEW EXERCISE 33

Match the word with its synonym.

___ 1.	quaint	a.	summarize
___ 2.	quarantine	b.	appease
___ 3.	quart	c.	odd
___ 4.	quilt	d.	loot
___ 5.	ransack	e.	avoid
___ 6.	realm	f.	majestic
___ 7.	recapitulate	g.	fix
___ 8.	reconcile	h.	bedspread
___ 9.	rectify	i.	dimension
___ 10.	refrain	j.	isolation
___ 11.	refute	k.	contradict
___ 12.	regal	l.	no synonym

From the words above, fill in the blanks with the most appropriate word. The word form may need changing.

1. You are _____ to prevent spreading the virus to the rest of the population.

2. The Queen's jewels and elegant dress gave her a _____ air.

3. Humans growing wings is not in the _____ of possibilities.

4. He tried to _____ with his estranged brother after many years.

5. You have to _____ from making noise at night because I can't sleep.

6. The thief _____ the house looking for cash and valuables.

7. Old theories are _____ all the time as technology progresses.

8. It is recommended to drink a _____ of water a day.

9. The construction workers visited the site to _____ the structural problems.

10. The _____ is made of colorful patches from different fabrics.

11. The _____ bed and breakfast is popular among tourists.

12. The professor would _____ the key points at the end of every lecture.

WORD SET 34

registration: [rej-uh-STREY-shuh n] Noun
The act of recording a name or other information on an official list.
A certificate attesting to the fact that someone or something has been registered.

- The **registration** to vote is very important.
- The **registration** of birth, death and marriage is normally a legal requirement.

Synonym: booking, certification, enrollment, filing
Antonym: none
Further Information
- Originated from the Latin word *re + gerere* meaning "back" + "carry or bear."
- **Registration** implies "officially being listed or recorded."

renegade: [REN-i-geyd] Noun/Adjective
A person who deserts a party or cause for another. (n.)
Of or like a renegade. (adj.)

- He was denounced as a **renegade** by the party. (n.)
- The **renegade** group returned to win the competition. (adj.)

Synonym: rebellious, reactionary, apostate, backsliding, dissident
Antonym: obedient
Further Information
- Originated from the Latin word *renegare* meaning "deny."
- **Traitor** evokes a stronger negative emotion than **renegade**.

repealed: [ri-PEEL d] Verb/Noun
To revoke or withdraw formally or officially. (v.)
The act of repealing. (n.)

- The proposal was promptly **repealed** by the directors. (v.)
- A **repeal** was announced by the parliament. (n.)

Synonym: abolish, abrogate, annul, cancel, dismantle, revoke
Antonym: allow, approve, build, enforce, establish
Further Information
- Originated from the Old French word *re + apeler* meaning "back" + "to call or appeal."
- **Repeal** is used when the decision is a law or a regulation. **R**evoke is used more generally.

replete: [ri-PLEET] Adjective
Abundantly supplied or provided.

- The garden is **replete** with homegrown vegetables.
- The essay is **replete** with filler words to make it longer than a page.

Synonym: full, awash, filled, loaded, rife
Antonym: empty, lacking, unfilled, wanting
<u>Further Information</u>
- Originated from the Latin word *re + plere* meaning "again" + "fill."
- **Replete** is an adjective and means "abundance and excess" while **deplete** is a verb and means "to empty or unload."

reprieve: [ri-PREEV] Verb/Noun
To delay the impending punishment or sentence of. (v.)
Any respite or temporary relief. (n.)

- The suspect was **reprieved** after new evidence emerged proving his innocence. (v.)
- The couple who faced eviction has been given a **reprieve**. (n.)

Synonym: abatement, absolution, amnesty, clemency, deferment
Antonym: continuation
<u>Further Information</u>
- Originated from the Middle French word *reprendre* meaning "take back."
- In Law, **reprieve** is "the temporary suspension or punishment while the situation is analyzed" while a **pardon** is "an official forgiveness."

reproach: [ri-PROHCH] Verb/Noun
To find fault with (a person, group, etc.) (v.)
Disgrace, discredit, or blame incurred. (n.)

- His mother **reproached** him for not taking his homework seriously. (v.)
- His actions resulted in **reproach** from his family. (n.)

Synonym: criticism, dishonor, disgrace
Antonym: approval, commendation, compliment
<u>Further Information</u>
- Originated from the Latin word *re + prope* meaning "opposite of" + "near."
- **Reproach** is "to express mild disapproval of an action" while **reprimand** is "to officially inform of one's disapproval."

residue: [REZ-i-dyoo] Noun
Something that remains after a part is removed, disposed of, or used.

- Please scrape the **residue** left in the pan.
- The **residue** of his estate was divided equally among them.

Synonym: leftover, debris, silt, slag
Antonym: base, core
Further Information
- Originated from the Latin word *residere* meaning "remain behind."
- **Residue** means "something that remains" while **residual** is "the quantity left over."

resistant: [ri-ZIS-tuh nt] Adjective
Not wanting to accept something, especially changes or new ideas.
Not harmed or affected by something.

- People are typically **resistant** to change unless there is a crisis.
- The specially treated wood was **resistant** to water.

Synonym: impervious to, unaffected by, immune to, unyielding
Antonym: receptive to, susceptible to
Further Information
- Originated from the Latin word *re + sistere* meaning "against" + "take a stand."
- **Resistant** implies "explicit unwillingness" while **hesitant** implies "uncertainty."

restricted: [ri-STRIK-tid] Adjective
To confine or keep within limits, as of space, action, choice, intensity, or quantity.

- The student was **restricted** from using too many chemicals during the experiment.
- Mom **restricted** us from spending too much when we went shopping.

Synonym: limited, barred, blocked, closed, confined
Antonym: free, unbound
Further Information
- Originated from the Latin word *re + stringere* meaning "back" + "draw tight."
- **Restricted** implies "to keep within limits" while **constricted** means "to tighten or put pressure."

retaliate: [ri-TAL-ee-eyt] Verb
To return like for like, especially evil for evil.

- Animals **retaliate** when hurt or attacked, especially mothers with a young one.
- It is only natural to want to **retaliate** when someone is mean.

Synonym: get even, reciprocate
Antonym: turn the other cheek
Further Information
- Originated from the Latin word *re + talis* means "back" + "such."
- **Retaliation** is a quick defensive reaction whereas **revenge** is "plotting to get even."

retract: [ri-TRAKT] Verb
To draw back within itself or oneself, fold up, or the like, or to be capable of doing this.
To withdraw (a statement, opinion, etc.) as inaccurate or unjustified, especially formally or explicitly.

- The blade can **retract** to its handle, making it portable.
- The witness **retracted** his previous statement under cross-examination.

Synonym: back down, cancel, deny, disavow, disown, withdraw
Antonym: acknowledge, admit, agree, allow, permit
Further Information
- Originated from the Latin word *re + trahere* meaning "back" + "drag."
- **Retract** is "to withdraw" while **redact** is "to censor/obscure."

retreat: [ri-TREET] Noun/Verb
The act of withdrawing, as into safety or privacy. (n.)
To withdraw, retire, or draw back, especially for shelter or seclusion. (v.)

- I am excited about going to the country **retreat** next weekend. (n.)
- The troops were forced to **retreat** as the enemy was stronger. (v.)

Synonym: departure, evacuation, flight, withdrawal, resort, sanctuary
Antonym: advance, arrival, coming
Further Information
- Originated from the Latin word *re + trahere* meaning "back" + "to draw."
- Should not be confused with **re-treat** which means "to treat again."

REVIEW EXERCISE 34

Match the word with its synonym.

___	1.	registration	a.		unyielding
___	2.	renegade	b.		criticism
___	3.	repealed	c.		dissident
___	4.	replete	d.		amnesty
___	5.	reprieve	e.		limited
___	6.	reproach	f.		debris
___	7.	residue	g.		withdraw
___	8.	resistant	h.		resort
___	9.	restricted	i.		filled
___	10.	retaliate	j.		get even
___	11.	retract	k.		booking
___	12.	retreat	l.		abolish

From the words above, fill in the blanks with the most appropriate word. The word form may need changing.

1. My new watch is water-_____ so I can go swimming without removing it.

2. The community _____ his leadership because of his dishonest actions.

3. There's a _____ required before you can join the workshop.

4. The weekend trip to the Bahamas _____ was relaxing and rejuvenating.

5. The forest is _____ with rare species of plants.

6. The _____ candidate joined the opposing party.

7. The governor _____ his earlier statement about putting up a new park.

8. Every day, I get a short _____ from work by taking a nap.

9. Non-authorized personnel are _____ from accessing that room.

10. Old laws are regularly _____ in court to make way for new ones.

11. Do not _____ when someone is violent and unreasonable; try to walk away.

12. _____ of coffee stains on a white shirt is difficult to remove with just plain soap.

WORD SET 35

revert: [ri-VURT] Verb
To return to a former habit, practice, belief, condition, etc.
A person or thing that reverts.

- He eventually **reverted** to the habit of eating junk food.
- He **reverts** to speaking in his native language when angry.

Synonym: degenerate, go back, react, regress
Antonym: develop
Further Information
- Originated from the Vulgar Latin word *re + vertere* meaning "back" + "to turn or bend."
- **Revert** implies "coming back to a position you were in earlier" while **reverse** is "to turn back or undo several actions."

ridge: [rij] Noun/Verb
A long, narrow elevation of land. (n.)
To provide with or form into a ridge or ridges. (v.)

- The camp is just over the **ridge**, a few kilometers away. (n.)
- The south area was **ridged** to prevent flooding. (v.)

Synonym: crest, fold, hill, ledge, crinkle
Antonym: smooth
Further Information
- Originated from the Old English word *hrycg* meaning "spine/crest."
- A **ridge** is "an elevation" while a **valley** is "a depression."

righteously: [RAHY-chuh s lee] Adverb
Characterized by uprightness or morality.

- Samantha is usually **righteously** indignant at anyone who breaks rules and regulations.
- Mother always told us to live **righteously** and kindly towards others.

Synonym: justly, accurately, correctly, decently, duly
Antonym: wrongly
Further Information
- Originated from the Old English word *riht + wis + ly* meaning "right" + "wise or manner" + adverb suffix for nouns.
- **Righteously** means "to uphold high standards of morality" while **rightfully** means "to have a valid or just claim."

riveting: [RIV-it-ing] Adjective
Completely engrossing.

- The movie has a **riveting** plot which is popular with young adults.
- She told a **riveting** tale about her adventures in Asia.

Synonym: fascinating, absorbing, captivating, compelling, enchanting
Antonym: boring, repellent, repulsive
Further Information
- Originated from the Old French word *river* meaning "to clench, or fix."
- **Riveting** evokes a stronger emotion than **interesting**.

ruthless: [ROOTH-lis] Adjective
Without pity or compassion.

- Prepare to face one of the most **ruthless** competitions at the annual sports day.
- The Roman gladiator was a **ruthless** fighter.

Synonym: unrelenting, savage, brutal, merciless, heartless
Antonym: calm, kind, friendly, human
Further Information
- Originated from the 14th century word *reuth + less* meaning "pity" + "lacking of."
- **Ruthless** implies "without pity or compassion" while **cruel** means "heartless or mean."

salient: [SEY-lee-uh nt] Adjective
Prominent or conspicuous.
Projecting or pointing outward.

- Her charm is one of her **salient** traits that attracts many admirers.
- The teacher highlighted the **salient** points of the presentation.

Synonym: noticeable, important, arresting, pertinent, weighty
Antonym: unimportant
Further Information
- Originated from the Latin word *salient* meaning "to leap."
- **Salient** implies "something that is clearly noticeable" while **important** implies "something of great significant."

sanction: [SANGK-shuh n] Noun/Verb
Penalty for disobeying law; Official permission. (n.)
To authorize, approve, or allow. (v.)

- The government gave **sanction** to build the new factory. (n.)
- The school will not **sanction** alcohol during the dance. (v.)

Synonym: penalty, punishment, approval, allowance, assent, authorize, allow
Antonym: reward, deny, disagree, disallow, oppose, protest
<u>Further Information</u>
- Originated from the Latin word *sancire* meaning "ratify."
- In Law, **sanctions** are penalties or punishments, as in "The United Nations imposed economic sanctions."

sanitary: [SAN-i-ter-ee] Adjective
Of or relating to health or the conditions affecting health, especially with reference to cleanliness, precautions against disease, etc.

- The chef always makes sure that the kitchen is **sanitary**.
- Hot, boiling water can be used to make pots **sanitary** for cooking.

Synonym: clean, healthful, hygienic, purified
Antonym: dirty, polluted, diseased, insanitary
<u>Further Information</u>
- Originated from the Latin word *sanus* meaning "healthy."
- **Sanitary** implies "removing waste or dirt" while **hygiene** refers to "the general habits of being clean."

satiated: [SEY-shee-ey-tid] Adjective
Satisfied, as one's appetite or desire, to the point of boredom.

- The large pizza that I had for lunch **satiated** my hunger quite well.
- Going out from time to time **satiated** Jeremy's need to socialize.

Synonym: gratify, indulge, nauseate, sate, slake
Antonym: disappoint, abstain
<u>Further Information</u>
- Originated from the Latin word *satis* meaning "enough."
- **Sated** is an almost exact synonym.

savvy: [SAV-ee] Adjective/Noun
Experienced, knowledgeable, and well-informed. (adj.)
Practical understanding. (n.)

- Sean is a tech-**savvy** businessman who uses different gadgets for work. (adj.)
- She has a lot of political **savvy** and knows how to deal with the media. (n.)

Synonym: shrewd, acute, cunning, discerning, keen
Antonym: blunt, coarse, dull, ignorant
<u>Further Information</u>
- Originated from the Spanish phrase *sabe usted* meaning "you know."
- **Savvy** is typically used informally.

scant: [skant] Adjective
Barely sufficient in amount or quantity.

- During summer, there is a **scant** supply of water.
- He paid **scant** attention to his health when he was younger.

Synonym: meager, insufficient, mere, paltry
Antonym: adequate, ample, enough, important, plentiful
<u>Further Information</u>
- Originated from the Old Norse word *skammr* meaning "short."
- **Scant** implies "very little" while **scarce** means "rare or lacking."

scarcity: [SKAIR-si-tee] Noun
Insufficiency or shortness of supply.

- There is a **scarcity** of food grains during a drought.
- The **scarcity** of space in cities caused rents to go up.

Synonym: dearth, drought, famine, inadequacy, insufficiency
Antonym: abundance, enough, excess, plenty
<u>Further Information</u>
- Originated from the Latin word *excerpere* meaning "pluck out."
- **Scarcity** implies "naturally occurring lack" while **shortage** implies "man-made lack."

REVIEW EXERCISE 35

Match the word with its synonym.

___	1. revert	a.	hill
___	2. ridge	b.	merciless
___	3. righteously	c.	cunning
___	4. riveting	d.	meager
___	5. ruthless	e.	justly
___	6. salient	f.	captivating
___	7. sanction	g.	important
___	8. sanitary	h.	punishment
___	9. satiated	i.	inadequacy
___	10. savvy	j.	sated
___	11. scant	k.	hygienic
___	12. scarcity	l.	regress

From the words above, fill in the blanks with the most appropriate word. The word form may need changing.

1. The _____ trader knew how to buy low and sell high.

2. There is a _____ supply of food because of the drought.

3. The dictator is a _____ leader who does not care about the citizens.

4. Jonah _____ to eating comfort food when he is stressed.

5. Hospitals are always _____ in order to prevent the spread of diseases.

6. The _____ play received a standing ovation from the audience.

7. The _____ of water in the desert means few plants can survive there.

8. One of the _____ landmarks in France is the Eiffel Tower.

9. Living _____ means following high standards and values.

10. Be careful when you reach the _____ as cracks began to appear last month.

11. The students were _____ for violating the curfew.

12. Bungee jumping _____ my thirst for an adrenaline rush.

WORD SET 36

scorn: [skawrn] Noun/Verb
Open or unqualified contempt. (n.)
To treat or regard with contempt or disdain. (v.)

- He felt **scorn** towards his rivals who cheated during the competition. (n.)
- Sammy **scorns** people who are uncaring. (v.)

Synonym: derision, disdain, mockery, ridicule, sarcasm
Antonym: flattery, praise, respect, compliment, approval
Further Information
- Originated from the Old French word *escarn* meaning "mockery or derision."
- Should not be confused with **scold** which means "to rebuke."

scornful: [SKAWRN-fuh l] Adjective
Feeling or expressing contempt or derision.

- The **scornful** remark was quite mean and unnecessary.
- He gave a **scornful** look to the innocent man.

Synonym: contemptuous, disdain, sneering, arrogant, cynical
Antonym: admiring, flattering, gracious, polite
Further Information
- Originated from the Old French word *escarn + ful* meaning "mockery or derision" + adjective suffix for noun.
- **Scornful** evokes a stronger negative emotion than **mocking**.

scrupulous: [SKROO-pyuh-luh s] Adjective
Having or showing a strict regard for what one considers right.
Punctiliously or minutely careful, precise, or exact.

- Jonah is considered a **scrupulous** student by his teachers.
- Her **scrupulous** attention to detail is an advantage.

Synonym: conscientious, cautious, careful, circumspect
Antonym: careless
Further Information
- Originated from the Latin word *scrupulus* meaning "pricking of conscience."
- The root word **scruple** means "a moral consideration or standard" or "a very small portion."

segregation: [seg-ri-GEY-shuh n]
A setting apart or separation of people or things from others or from the main body or group.

- **Segregation** of vehicles and pedestrians in the town center led to fewer accidents.
- In some countries, there is **segregation** between men and women.

Synonym: separation, apartheid, discrimination, isolation, partition
Antonym: connection
<u>Further Information</u>
- Originated from the Latin word *se + grex* meaning "apart" + "flock."
- In History, **segregation** means "the institutional separation of an ethnic, racial, religious, or other minority group from the dominant majority."

self-esteem: [SELF-i-STEEM]
A realistic respect for or favorable impression of oneself.

- Good **self-esteem** is a sign of sound mental health and well-being.
- Failure and defeat can lead to poor **self-esteem**.

Synonym: pride, confidence, dignity, morale, self-respect
Antonym: self-deprecation
<u>Further Information</u>
- Originated from the Old English word *self* + the French word *estimer* meaning "oneself" + "account or value."
- **Self-esteem** is "the belief in self-worth" while **self-efficac**y is "the belief in capacity to accomplish a task."

serpent: [SUR-puh nt] Noun
A snake.
A wily, treacherous, or malicious person.

- Be careful of the **serpents** on the forest floor, as some of them are poisonous.
- I believe there is a **serpent** in the group spying on our plans.

Synonym: snake, viper
Antonym: none
<u>Further Information</u>
- Originated from the Latin word *serpentem* meaning "snake or creeping thing."
- **Snake** is more commonly used in spoken English while **serpent** can usually be found in written works.

severed: [SEV-erd] Verb
To separate (a part) from the whole, as by cutting or the like.
To become separated from each other.

- He **severed** his artery in the accident and needed blood transfusion.
- He's trying to rebuild their **severed** relationship after so many years.

Synonym: cut, detach, disassociate, separate, split
Antonym: attach, combine, connect, couple
Further Information
- Originated from the Latin word *separare* meaning "disjoin or divide."
- **Severed** should *not* be confused as the past tense form of **severe** which means "harsh or extreme."

shambles: [SHAM-buh lz] Noun
A slaughterhouse.
Any scene, place, or thing in disorder.

- The north district is composed of **shambles** and meat shops.
- The coastline is in **shambles** after the storm hit yesterday.

Synonym: mess, disarray, anarchy, bedlam, chaos
Antonym: calm, harmony, order
Further Information
- Originated from the Latin word *scamnum* meaning "bench."
- **Shamble** can also mean "to walk awkwardly."

shrewd: [shrood] Adjective
Astute or sharp in practical matters.

- The city elected a **shrewd** mayor who managed to rejuvenate the economy.
- Janny is known to be a **shrewd** and decisive decision-maker.

Synonym: clever, intelligent, crafty, astute, keen
Antonym: blunt, dull, foolish, honest, idiotic
Further Information
- Originated from the 13th century word *shrewe* meaning "wicked man."
- **Shrewd** may sometimes refer to "cunning" with negative undertones.

shrill: [shril] Adjective/Verb
High-pitched and piercing in sound quality. (adj.)
To make a shrill noise. (v.)

- The loud, **shrill** siren indicates serious emergency. (adj.)
- A piercing whistle **shrilled** through the night air. (v.)

Synonym: high-pitched, discordant, deafening, noisy, piercing
Antonym: clam, low, mild, moderate, quiet
Further Information
- Originated from the Low German word *schrell* meaning "sharp in tone or taste."
- **Shrill** implies "an irritating sound."

shun: [shuhn] Verb
To keep away from (a place, person, object, etc.) due to dislike, caution, etc.

- Sammy **shuns** crowded places such as the train station.
- You need to eat healthy and **shun** junk food and soda.

Synonym: avoid, ignore, despise, disdain, eschew
Antonym: accept, admire, allow, approve, cherish
Further Information
- Originated from the Old English word *scunian* meaning "abhor."
- **Shun** implies a stronger desire to avoid than **ignore**.

sincere: [sin-SEER] Adjective
Free of deceit, hypocrisy, or falseness.

- The audience was captivated by his **sincere** performance.
- Sammy values her **sincere** friendship with Bea.

Synonym: honest, candid, earnest, forthright, genuine
Antonym: counterfeit, deceitful, devious, dishonest, false
Further Information
- Originated from the Latin word *sincerus* meaning "clean or pure."
- **Sincere** implies "heartfelt" while **authentic** means "original/genuine."

REVIEW EXERCISE 36

Match the word with its synonym.

___	1.	scorn	a.	sneering
___	2.	scornful	b.	discrimination
___	3.	scrupulous	c.	snake
___	4.	segregation	d.	disarray
___	5.	self-esteem	e.	disdain
___	6.	serpent	f.	detach
___	7.	severed	g.	avoid
___	8.	shambles	h.	confidence
___	9.	shrewd	i.	piercing
___	10.	shrill	j.	clever
___	11.	shun	k.	cautious
___	12.	sincere	l.	honest

From the words above, fill in the blanks with the most appropriate word. The word form may need changing.

1. The house was in _____ after the party because no one bothered to clean up.

2. Bob is known to be a _____ accountant who double checks his works all the time.

3. Victoria's _____ apology was well received by her friend.

4. Manuel is _____ of anyone who disagrees with him.

5. The power lines were _____ during the storm resulting in darkness in many

   parts of the county.

6. The child's _____cry alerted his parents so they rushed to check on him.

7. The _____ based on ethnicity was opposed by the civil rights movement.

8. The governor ignored the _____ of some citizens who picketed outside his office.

9. Low _____ is the cause of many difficulties in career and life.

10. Some celebrities _____ extreme publicity and consider it unnecessary for their career.

11. Please catch the _____ crawling on the floor.

12. Monica is a _____ planner who prepares for everything.

WORD SET 37

sinuous: [SIN-yoo-uh s] Adjective
Having many curves, bends, or turns.
Characterized by a series of graceful curving motions.

- Follow the **sinuous** path down the mountain to the next camp.
- The **sinuous** movement of a snake is quite fascinating.

Synonym: winding, twisting, crooked, curved, meandering, Supple, agile
Antonym: straight, clumsy
Further Information
- Originated from the Latin word *sinus* meaning "a bend."
- **Meandering** implies a more curved movement than **sinuous**.

smother: [SMUHTH-er] Verb
To stifle or suffocate, to prevent free breathing; To be overly protective;
To suppress (a feeling or action); To cover something entirely;
To extinguish or deaden (fire, coals, etc.) by covering so as to exclude air.

- The intense heat and humidity **smothered** the travelers.
- Make sure to **smother** the campfire before you go to sleep.

Synonym: extinguish, cover, choke, douse, envelop, overwhelm, inundate, stifle, smear
Antonym: allow, encourage, free, help
Further Information
- Originated from the Old English word *smorian* meaning "suffocate."
- Should not be confused with **smoother** which means "free from unevenness."

sneering: [sneer-ing] Adjective/Noun
Rude and not showing respect. (adj.)
A facial expression of scorn or contempt. (n.)

- Ben's **sneering** reply was surprising to everyone. (adj.)
- Her **sneering** turned everyone against her during the project. (n.)

Synonym: scoffing, contemptible, derisive, sarcastic
Antonym: admiring
Further Information
- Originated from the North Frisian word *sneere* meaning "to scorn."
- **Sneering** often refers to facial expressions while **scorn** refers to emotions.

snivel: [SNIV-uh l] Verb/Noun
To weep or cry with sniffling; To complain in a tearful way. (v.)
The act or sound of snivelling. (n.)

- I heard her **snivel** while watching the emotional TV drama. (v.)
- The horse's **snivel** could mean it's in pain or is sick. (n.)

Synonym: complain, cry, gripe, groan, whimper
Antonym: none
<u>Further Information</u>
- Originated from the Old English word *snyflan* meaning "to run at the nose."
- **Snivel** may also mean "one having a runny nose or having a cold."

sodden: [SOD-n] Adjective/Verb
Soaked in liquid or moisture. (adj.)
To make or become sodden. (v.)

- Nobody likes eating **sodden** cereals in the morning. (adj.)
- Could you **sodden** the frozen meat so we can put it on the grill later? (v.)

Synonym: saturated, soaked, soggy, drenched, steeped
Antonym: arid, dry
<u>Further Information</u>
- Originated from the Old English word *soden* meaning "boiled."
- **Sodden** implies being more soaked than **soggy**.

solace: [SOL-is] Noun/Verb
Comfort in sorrow, misfortune, or trouble. (n.)
To comfort, console, or cheer. (v.)

- The donation was a **solace** to the grieving family. (n.)
- A lonely heart can be **solaced** by having company. (v.)

Synonym: comfort, peace, condolence, pity, consolation
Antonym: none
<u>Further Information</u>
- Originated from the Latin word *solari* meaning "to console."
- **Comfort** refers to the "feeling of general contentment" while **solace** refers to "bringing comfort in time of distress."

sole: [sohl] Adjective/Noun
Being the only one. (adj.)
Under-surface or a person's foot; underside of footwear. (n.)
A marine flatfish used as food. (n.)

- The soles of their feet were nearly black with dirt. (n.)
- John is the **sole** male in the art and craft workshop. (adj.)

Synonym: alone, unique, remaining, individual, bottom
Antonym: common, both, together
Further Information
- Originated from the Latin word *solus* meaning "alone."
- Should not be confused with **soul** which has the same pronunciation.

solvent: [sol-vuh nt] Adjective/Noun
Having the power of dissolving: able to pay all just debts. (adj.)
A substance that dissolves another to form a solution. (n.)

- Sammy worked hard to keep his company **solvent**. (adj.)
- Water is considered the universal **solvent**, as almost everything dissolves in it. (n.)

Synonym: financially sound, debt-free, secure, dissolver, solution
Antonym: in-debt, insolvent
Further Information
- Originated from the French word *solvere* meaning "to loosen or accomplish."
- **Solvent** is the substance used to dissolve while **solute** is the substance to be dissolved.

sophisticated: [suh-FIS-ti-key-tid] Adjective
Altered by education, experience, etc., so as to be worldly-wise.
Complex or intricate, as a system, process, piece of machinery, or the like.

- Samantha is considered well-travelled and **sophisticated** by her peers.
- The **sophisticated** solution works well when implemented properly.

Synonym: cultured, mature, refined, complex, advanced
Antonym: unrefined, unsophisticated, harsh, simple
Further Information
- Originated from the Medieval Latin word *sophisticus* meaning "cultured."
- The word **sophisticate** refers to a person who is **sophisticated**.

spanner: [SPAN-er] Noun
A wrench having a curved head with a hook or pin at one end for engaging notches or holes in collars.
A source of impediment or annoyance.

- Father asked you to fetch his **spanner** in the garage.
- The lack of funds for the project threw a **spanner** in the works.

Synonym: wrench
Antonym: none
Further Information
- Originated from the German word *spannen* meaning "to join, fasten, extend, connect."
- Wrench is mostly used in North America, as in "throw a wrench in the works."
- In UK English, **spanner** also means "a source of impediment or annoyance."

sparse: [spahrs] Adjective
Thinly scattered or distributed; In short supply.

- The **sparse** food supply had to be carefully rationed.
- There were many areas of **sparse** population in the desert country.

Synonym: inadequate, infrequent, meager, scant, scarce
Antonym: abundant, adequate, enough, fat, frequent
Further Information
- Originated from the Latin word *spargere* meaning "scatter."
- The direct opposite of **sparse** is dense.

spearhead: [SPEER-hed] Noun/Verb
Any person, contingent, or force that leads an attack, undertaking, etc. (n.)
To act as a spearhead for. (v.)

- Allied troops formed the **spearhead** of the attack. (n.)
- I was asked by the boss to **spearhead** the next project. (v.)

Synonym: lead, start, initiate, launch, prompt
Antonym: end, finish, stop
Further Information
- First used in the 1300s as a Middle English word combining **spear + head.**
- Literally, **spearhead** means "the sharp-pointed head that forms the piercing end of a spear."

REVIEW EXERCISE 37

Match the word with its synonym.

___	1.	sinuous	a.	firm
___	2.	smother	b.	cultured
___	3.	sneering	c.	winding
___	4.	snivel	d.	wrench
___	5.	sodden	e.	comfort
___	6.	solace	f.	alone
___	7.	sole	g.	scoffing
___	8.	solvent	h.	douse
___	9.	sophisticated	i.	scant
___	10.	spanner	j.	lead
___	11.	sparse	k.	cry
___	12.	spearhead	l.	wet

From the words above, fill in the blanks with the most appropriate word. The word form may need changing.

1.   Put your _____ clothes in the dryer before you go to your room.

2.   Bees use a _____ method of communicating which allows them to work efficiently.

3.   People are _____ at his unconventional methods of teaching.

4.   The _____ movement of the snake through the grass field means it's stalking

     a prey.

5.   I found _____ in working for a charity where I can help many people.

6.   Traffic in the countryside is _____ because we use bicycles.

7.   It is difficult to _____ a very large project without adequate support.

8.   The company is _____ and able to pay its debts and loans.

9.   Make sure to _____ the fire before leaving the camp.

10. The _____ beneficiary of the grant received a large amount of money.

11. We were planning an outdoor event but the bad weather threw a _____ in the works.

12. The bully left his victim _____ on the ground.

WORD SET 38

sphere: [sfeer] Noun
A round solid figure.
The place or environment within which a person or thing exists.

- The investor's **sphere** of influence was limited to the company directors.
- The glass **spheres** in the chandelier look good especially when the lights are on.

Synonym: globe, circle, orb, field, realm
Antonym: none
Further Information
- Originated from the Greek word *sphaira* meaning "ball."
- **Sphere** is archaically used as a verb. Now, we use **circle** as in "circle your answers in the test."

spire: [spahyuhr] Noun/Verb
A tall, acutely pointed pyramidal roof or roof-like construction upon a tower, roof, etc. (n.)
Rise or extend to a height in the manner of a spire. (v.)

- The **spires** of the mountains can be seen from the town. (n.)
- He **spired** into the peak of his career at a very early age. (v.)

Synonym: tower, steeple, apex, peak, pinnacle, cone
Antonym: base, bottom
Further Information
- Originated from the Old English word *spir* meaning "tall, slender stem of a plant."
- A **steeple** is often a tall tower on a building while **spire** is a conical structure on top of it.

spoof: [spoof] Noun/Verb
A mocking imitation of someone or something, usually light and good-humored. (n.)
To mock (something or someone) lightly and good-humoredly. (v.)

- The movie is a **spoof** on office life in an IT company. (n.)
- His career is mostly **spoofing** movie actors and other celebrities. (v.)

Synonym: lampoon, tricky, mockery, satire, prank, parody
Antonym: frankness, honesty, openness
Further Information
- **Spoof** was coined by the English comedian Arthur Roberts.
- **Spoof** implies humor while **mockery** is more offensive.

sporadically: [spuh-rad-ik lee] Adverb
(Of similar things or occurrences) Appearing or happening at irregular intervals in time.

- They met **sporadically** over the course of two years.
- The scientist **sporadically** recorded the changes in the experiment.

Synonym: intermittently, infrequently, occasionally, rarely, seldom
Antonym: frequently, regularly, usually
Further Information
- Originated from the Greek word *sporas + ly* meaning "scattered" + adverb suffix for adjectives.
- **Sporadically** implies "seldom and irregular."

springboard: [SRING-bawrd] Noun
A flexible board, projecting over water, from which divers leap or spring.
Something that supplies the impetus or conditions for a beginning, change, or progress.

- He still hasn't fixed the **springboard** in the swimming area.
- Being a lawyer can be a **springboard** to a political career.

Synonym: jump off, beginning, venture, starting, launch-pad
Antonym: none
Further Information
- Originated from *spring + board* meaning "start of" + "plank."
- **Springboard** implies "starting point."

spurn: [spurn] Verb
To reject with disdain or contempt.

- Mickey **spurned** the offer of seafood due to his allergy.
- He spoke with hesitation as if afraid that his invitation would be **spurned**.

Synonym: ignore, despise, disdain, dismiss, disregard
Antonym: accept, admire, allow, approve, include
Further Information
- Originated from the Latin word *spernere* meaning "to scorn."
- **Scorn** implies "feeling of contempt" while **spurn** implies "display of contempt."

squabble: [SKWOB-uh l] Verb/Noun
To engage in a petty quarrel. (v.)
A petty quarrel. (n.)

- They **squabble** over the shallowest things all the time. (v.)
- Do not let a **squabble** last or it will create big problems in your relationship. (n.)

Synonym: argument, bickering, different, dispute, feud, quarrel
Antonym: accord, agreement, harmony, peace
Further Information
- Originated from the Dialectical German word *schwabbeln* meaning "to talk foolishly."
- **Squabble** often implies "loud and noisy quarrel."

squander: [SKWON-der] Verb
To spend or use (money, time, etc.) extravagantly or wastefully.

- He **squandered** his allowance on candy and chocolate.
- The team **squandered** several chances to score.

Synonym: blow, expend, lavish, misuse, waste
Antonym: hoard, save, accumulate, collect
Further Information
- Coined in the 1500s and used by Shakespeare in his works to imply "spending recklessly."
- **Squander** implies "to waste resources" while **splurge** means "extravagant display."

stampede: [stam-PEED] Noun/Verb
A sudden, frenzied rush or headlong flight of a herd of frightened animals or humans. (n.)
To scatter or flee in a stampede. (v.)

- It was fascinating to see a huge **stampede** of animals in Africa. (n.)
- People **stampeded** during the fire which led to more injuries. (v.)

Synonym: panic, charge, chase, dash, flight
Antonym: retreat, standing
Further Information
- Originated from the Spanish word *estamper* meaning "to stamp or press."
- **Stampeded** often implies "panic."

stethoscope: [STETH-uh-skohp] Noun
An instrument used to convey sounds in the chest or other parts of the body to the ear of the examiner.

- A **stethoscope** is used by the doctor to listen to your internal organs.
- Doctor Shaw is forgetful and seems to lose his **stethoscope** all the time.

Synonym: cardiograph
Antonym: none
Further Information
- Originated from the Greek word *stethos + scope* meaning "chest" + word forming element indicating "an instrument for seeing."
- **Stethoscope** is often used to listen to the lungs or heart.

stowaway: [STOH-uh-wey] Noun
A person who hides aboard a ship or airplane in order to obtain free transportation or elude pursuers.

- The tight security in airports is also to scare off **stowaways**.
- The child dreamt about being a **stowaway** in a pirate ship.

Synonym: hide
Antonym: none
Further Information
- Originated from the Old English word *sto + aweg* meaning "to pack" + "from this place."
- The phrasal verb **stow away** means to "put away."

strum: [struhm] Verb/Noun
To play on (a stringed musical instrument) by running the fingers lightly across the strings. (v.)
The sound produced by strumming. (n.)

- **Strum** the guitar to hear if it is in tune or not. (v.)
- The guitarist's **strum** was quite complex which impressed the judges. (n.)

Synonym: tweak, pluck
Antonym: end, finish, stop
Further Information
- First used in the 17th century, meaning to "run fingers across a string instrument."

REVIEW EXERCISE 38

Match the word with its synonym.

___ 1.   sphere   a.   pluck
___ 2.   spire   b.   panic
___ 3.   spoof   c.   bicker
___ 4.   sporadically   d.   parody
___ 5.   springboard   e.   hide
___ 6.   spurn   f.   tower
___ 7.   squabble   g.   expend
___ 8.   squander   h.   dismiss
___ 9.   stampede   i.   circle
___ 10. stethoscope   j.   intermittently
___ 11. stowaway   k.   launch pad
___ 12. strum   l.   cardiograph

From the words above, fill in the blanks with the most appropriate word. The word form may need changing.

1.   The busker is softly _____ his guitar along with the river

2.   The crew discovered a _____ hiding in one of the ship's compartments.

3.   The directors _____ his suggestion for creating a new department.

4.   Howard will not _____ his savings on flashy cars or fancy boats.

5.   Working for a start-up company is his _____ to setting up his own business.

6.   Some comedy shows are _____ of real life situations.

7.   In the remote islands, Internet service was _____ and unreliable.

8.   Developed countries have a large _____ of international influence.

9.   The gymnasium was designed to avoid a _____ during emergencies.

10. The doctor used his _____ to check if I have pneumonia.

11. The _____ on top of the church is being renovated.

12. Sometimes mom and dad _____ over silly things.

WORD SET 39

subside: [suh b-SAHYD] Verb
To sink to a low or lower level.
To become quiet, less active, or less violent.

- The flood is beginning to **subside** after weeks of rain.
- Your headache will **subside** in a couple of hours if you take this medicine.

Synonym: slacken, ebb, wane, dwindle, ease
Antonym: increase, grow, enlarge, prolong, ascend
Further Information
- Originated from the Latin word *sub + sidere* meaning "below" + "settle."
- **Subside** means "to sink or fall" while **subdue** means "to quieten or bring under control."

succulent: [SUHK-yuh-luh nt] Adjective/Noun
Full of juice. (adj.)
A succulent plant. (n.)

- The dish was so **succulent** she asked for a second serving. (adj.)
- Cactus is considered a **succulent** because of its fleshy leaves. (n.)

Synonym: moist, luscious, tasty, yummy, lush
Antonym: dry
Further Information
- Originated from the Latin word *succus* meaning "juice."
- **Succulent** implies "delicious and juicy."

sugarcoat: [SHOOG-er-koht] Verb
To make (something difficult or distasteful) appear more pleasant or acceptable.
To cover with sugar.

- The bitter pill was **sugarcoated** to make it more palatable.
- Alana does not **sugarcoat** anything she says.

Synonym: glaze, sweeten, candy
Antonym: sour, displease
Further Information
- Originated from the Old French word *sucre + cote* meaning "sugar" + "coat or robe."
- **Sugarcoat** implies "to make something sound nice and may involve lying."

suppress: [suh-PRES] Verb
To put an end to the activities of (a person, body of persons, etc.)
To do away with authority.

- He **suppressed** his laughter during his presentation.
- Government should never **suppress** freedom of speech.

Synonym: subdue, quench, censor, curb, repress
Antonym: release, permit, sanction, aid, assist
Further Information
- Originated from the Latin word *sub + premere* meaning "down" + "to press."
- **Oppress** is to "consciously keep someone down by unjust authority" while **suppress** is a more general term meaning "to inhibit or put an end to."

surplus: [SUR-pluhs] Noun/Adjective
An amount, quantity, etc., greater than needed. (n.)
Being in excess of what is required. (adj.)

- The country exported its food **surplus**. (n.)
- During spring, farmers sell **surplus** crops directly to people. (adj.)

Synonym: extra, excess, leftover, unused
Antonym: essential, lacking, necessary
Further Information
- Originated from the Medieval Latin word *super + plus* meaning "in addition" + "more."
- **Surplus** implies "something extra or unused available cheaply."

swivel: [SWIV-uh l] Noun/Verb
A device consisting of two parts, each of which turns around independently. (n.)
To turn or pivot on a swivel. (v.)

- The carpenter installed a **swivel** to the bookshelf for the hidden room. (n.)
- She **swiveled** in her seat and fell on the ground. (v.)

Synonym: spin, pivot, revolve, rotate, swing around, whirl
Antonym: stationary
Further Information
- Originated from the Old English word *swifan* meaning "to move or sweep."
- As nouns, a **swivel** is "a mechanism that allows movement" while a **pivot** is "something on which a thing turns."

sycophant: [SIK-uh-fuhnt]/[SAHy-kuh-fuhnt] Noun
A self-seeking flatterer.

- You don't want to be known as a **sycophant** at work.
- Politicians can sometimes be **sycophants**.

Synonym: toady, creep, flatterer
Antonym: none
<u>Further Information</u>
- Originated from the Greek word *sukon + phainein* meaning "fig" + "to show."
- A **sycophant** is someone who is "not sincere."

synthesis: [SIN-thuh-sis] Noun
The combining of the constituent elements of separate material or abstract entities into a single or unified entity.

- The famous painting was a **synthesi**s of different types of ancient arts.
- The **synthesis** of their ideas created a more compelling solution.

Synonym: combining, fusion, amalgam, blend, integration
Antonym: division, separation
<u>Further Information</u>
- Originated from the Greek word *suntithenai* meaning "place together."
- In Chemistry, **synthesis** is "the forming or building of a more complex substance or compound from elements or simpler compounds."

synthetic: [sin-THET-ik] Adjective
Pertaining to a substance formed through a chemical process.
Insincere action or emotion.

- His shoes made of **synthetic** leather look as good as genuine leather shoes.
- Their tears were a bit **synthetic**.

Synonym: artificial, fabricated, manufactured
Antonym: genuine, real, natural
<u>Further Information</u>
- Originated from the Greek word *suntithenai* meaning "place together."
- **Synthetic** implies "something that does not occur naturally."

tactful: [TAKT-fuh l] Adjective
Having or showing sensitivity in dealing with others.

- Hank is a **tactful** person whom everybody likes.
- Her **tactful** reply helped calm the customer down.

Synonym: thoughtful, careful, polite, courteous, discreet
Antonym: careless, foolish, impolite, incautious, tactless
Further Information
- Originated from the Latin word *tangere* meaning "to touch."
- **Tactful** is sometimes misspelled as **tactfull**.

tantalize: [TAN-tl-ahyz] Verb
To torment with, or as if with, the sight of something desired but out of reach.

- The store **tantalizes** its customers with a beautiful window display.
- Don't **tantalize** your brother with junk food.

Synonym: provoke, annoy, baffle, entice, titillate
Antonym: aid, assist, disenchant, encourage
Further Information
- Originated from the Greek word *tantalus + ize*, which is the name of the king of Phrygia + a verb forming suffix.
- **Tantalize** is also spelled as **tantalise**.

tarnish: [TAHR-nish] Verb/Noun
To diminish or destroy the purity of. (v.)
A stain or blemish. (n.)

- The accusation might **tarnish** his stellar career. (v.)
- A **tarnish** is hard to remove from silverware. (n.)

Synonym: dirty, corrupt, damage, defame, dim
Antonym: aid, assist, benefit, clean, fix
Further Information
- Originated from the French word *terne* meaning "dark or dull."
- Should not be confused with **varnish** which means "superficial polish or external show, especially to conceal some defect or inadequacy."

REVIEW EXERCISE 39

Match the word with its synonym.

___	1.	subside	a.	subdue
___	2.	succulent	b.	entice
___	3.	sugar coat	c.	sweeten
___	4.	suppress	d.	luscious
___	5.	surplus	e.	lackey
___	6.	swivel	f.	careful
___	7.	sycophant	g.	leftover
___	8.	synthesis	h.	pivot
___	9.	synthetic	i.	wane
___	10.	tactful	j.	damage
___	11.	tantalize	k.	fusion
___	12.	tarnish	l.	artificial

From the words above, fill in the blanks with the most appropriate word. The word form may need changing.

1. _____bad news will not fix the underlying issue.

2. The river waters rose after the storm yesterday, but have since _____.

3. The controversy can _____ the reputation of the prime minister.

4. The fur coat he's wearing is actually made of _____ materials.

5. The dictator is surrounded by _____ who can't say "no" to him.

6. The _____ fruit looks very delicious and juicy.

7. It is important to be _____ when discussing sensitive topics.

8. I sold my _____ clothes to the thrift store.

9. Mike _____ his frustration and apologized to the angry customer.

10. She _____ the chair around to face us.

11. Her novels are a rich _____ of history and mythology.

12. He _____ the kitten with fish.

WORD SET 40

tarnished: [TAHR-nish] Verb
To dull the lustre of (a metallic surface), especially by oxidation.
To diminish or destroy the purity of.

- The food we served today **tarnished** some of the china.
- Politicians do everything to avoid having a **tarnished** reputation.

Synonym: corrupted, damaged
Antonym: aided, assisted, benefited, cleaned, fixed
Further Information
- Originated from the French word *terne* meaning "dark or dull."
- In Chemistry, **tarnish** is "a thin layer of corrosion that forms over copper, brass, silver, aluminium, magnesium and other similar metals."

temperate: [TEM-per-it] Adjective
Moderate or self-restrained.
Climate characterized by milt temperature.

- I want to go back to the Caribbean where the weather is **temperate**.
- He is **temperate** in his consumption of food.

Synonym: calm, moderate, controlled, sober, balmy
Antonym: harsh, hateful, extreme, unpleasant, excessive
Further Information
- Originated from the Latin word *temperatus* meaning "restrained or moderate."
- **Temperate** is often used to describe the weather or climate of a region.

tempestuous: [tem-PES-choo-uh s] Adjective
Of or relating to strong and conflicting emotions.
Violent or stormy.

- The captain avoids sailing during **tempestuous** weather.
- After years of a **tempestuous** relationship, they finally separated.

Synonym: wild, stormy, heated, impassioned, passionate
Antonym: apathetic, calm, cool, indifferent, unexcited
Further Information
- Originated from the Latin word *tempestus* meaning "storm or commotion."
- **Tempestuous** implies "chaotic and disorganized."

tentative: [TEN-tuh-tiv] Adjective
Of the nature of or made or done as a trial, experiment, or attempt.
Unsure; Uncertain; Not definite or positive.

- Due to the storm, the plane's departure time was **tentative**.
- He's **tentative** when it comes to life-altering decisions.

Synonym: conditional, experimental, unsettled, indefinite, uncertain
Antonym: certain, conclusive, decisive, definite
Further Information
- Originated from the Medieval Latin word *temptare* meaning "handle or try."
- **Tentative** is often misspelled as **tenative** which is not a word.

terse: [turs] Adjective
Neatly or effectively concise.
Abruptly concise; Curt.

- Mindy's **terse** reply tells me that she is upset.
- His emails are usually **terse**, which can be confusing.

Synonym: brief, short, brusque, concise, curt
Antonym: gentle, kind, lengthy, long-winded
Further Information
- Originated from the Latin word *tergere* meaning "to rub or polish."
- **Terse** usually stems from strong and intense negative emotion.

thaw: [thaw] Verb/Noun
To pass or change from a frozen to a liquid or semi-liquid state; to become less hostile or tense. (v.)
A period of warmer weather that thaws ice and snow. (n.)

- A frozen turkey may take up to two days to **thaw**. (v.)
- The **thaw** came yesterday and children could finally go out and play. (n.)

Synonym: unfreeze, defrost, loosen
Antonym: coagulate, solidify
Further Information
- Originated from the Proto-Germanic word *thawon* meaning "to melt or dissolve."
- **Thaw** is typically used for food items or smaller objects while **defrost** is commonly used for machinery or bigger objects.

thistle: [this-uh l] Noun
Any of various prickly, composite plants having showy, purple flower heads.

- Avoid picking out the **thistle** I planted in the garden.
- **Thistle** is the national emblem of Scotland.

Synonym: barb, bramble, thorn, dart, prickle
Antonym: none
Further Information
- Originated from the Proto-Germanic word *thistilaz* meaning "to prick or pierce."
- **Thistle** is used on the badges of some sports teams.

thriving: [thrahy-ving] Verb
Be fortunate or successful.
To grow or develop vigorously.

- Jamie is **thriving** in the financial industry due to her Math skills.
- The tropical plants are **thriving** in hot and humid weather.

Synonym: successful, developing, flourishing, growing, healthy
Antonym: failing, infirm, poor, unhealthy
Further Information
- Originated from the Old Norse word *thrifa* meaning "grasp or get hold of."
- **Thriving** may also mean "significant growth towards betterment."

tiller: [TIL-er] Noun
An implement or machine for breaking up soil.
A horizontal bar fitted to the head of a boat's rudder post and used as a lever for steering.

- The farmer is using a **tiller** to plow the fields.
- Hold the **tiller** tightly while steering the boat so you can control it.

Synonym: shaft, stem, knob, wheel
Antonym: none
Further Information
- Originated from the Latin word *tela* meaning "web."
- **Tiller** may also mean "a person who tills; a farmer."

tournament: [TOOR-nuh-muh nt] Noun
A meeting for contests in a variety of sports, as between teams of different nations etc.

- He won the chess **tournament** yesterday.
- The Olympics is one of the biggest **tournaments** in the world.

Synonym: competition, contest, event, fight, match
Antonym: none
<u>Further Information</u>
- Originated from the Old French word *torneier* meaning "take part in a tourney."
- A **tournament** implies a bigger event than a **game** or a **competition**.

tow bar: [tow-bahr] Noun
A metal bar for attaching a vehicle to a load to be towed.

- Make sure to pack the **tow bar** in case the car breaks down.
- The traffic police are attaching the **tow bar** to the car.

Synonym: none
Antonym: none
<u>Further Information</u>
- **Tow bar** is the combination of the verb **tow** meaning "to pull" and the noun **bar** meaning "a rod."
- An alternative spelling to **tow bar** is **towbar**.

trinket: [TRING-kit] Noun
A small ornament, piece of jewelry, etc.

- The little girl collects shiny **trinkets** because they look pretty.
- Grandma likes giving away **trinkets** during Christmas.

Synonym: knickknack, bauble, bead, curio, jewelry
Antonym: none
<u>Further Information</u>
- **Trinket** implies "a small ornament of little or no value."
- Some synonyms of **trinket**, such as **doodad**, **gewgaw** and **bagatelle**, are used regionally.

REVIEW EXERCISE 40

Match the word with its synonym.

___	1.	tarnished	a.	curt
___	2.	temperate	b.	unfreeze
___	3.	tempestuous	c.	stormy
___	4.	tentative	d.	moderate
___	5.	terse	e.	successful
___	6.	thaw	f.	bauble
___	7.	thistle	g.	competition
___	8.	thriving	h.	barb
___	9.	tiller	i.	shaft
___	10.	tournament	j.	damaged
___	11.	trinket	k.	conditional
___	12.	towbar	l.	no synonym

From the words above, fill in the blanks with the most appropriate word. The word form may need changing.

1. The _____ economy created many jobs in different industries.

2. Some theories are _____ because they have not been fully reviewed.

3. His tone was _____ because he was not happy with the situation.

4. There are cheap _____ in the toy shop perfect for giveaways.

5. The new puppy's demeanor is more _____ than others of the same breed.

6. Their _____ relationship lasted for only a short while.

7. I fell on a thorny _____ bush and wounded myself.

8. We still have to wait for spring for the snow to _____.

9. They have to replace the broken _____ of the boat.

10. The new car was _____ with mud and gunk from the sewer.

11. Julie is hoping to win the _____ this year.

12. We need the _____ to pull the broken car to the side of the road.

WORD SET 41

trite: [trahyt] Adjective
Lacking in freshness or effectiveness because of constant use or excessive repetition.
Characterized by hackneyed expressions, ideas, etc.

- The movie's plot was **trite** and boring.
- The speech was long and filled with **trite** clichés.

Synonym: silly, commonplace, banal, corny, dull
Antonym: fresh, new, original
Further Information
- Originated from the Latin word *terere* meaning "to rub."
- **Trite** is typically misspelled as **tright** which is not a word.

trough: [trof] Noun
A long, narrow, open container for animals to eat/drink from.
A channel or conduit for conveying water, as a gutter under the eaves of a building for carrying away rain water.

- Make sure that the **trough** for the horses is always filled with clean water.
- The **trough** on the roof is clogged with dried leaves.

Synonym: gutter, depression, trench, canal, channel
Antonym: none
Further Information
- Originated from the Old English word *trog* meaning "wooden vessel, tray or hollow."
- **Trough** may also refer to "a depression or the lowest point."

unadorned: [uhn-uh-DAWRND] Adjective
Without frills; plain.

- News writers often prefer **unadorned** writing styles.
- The office building is very plain with its walls **unadorned**.

Synonym: plain, simple, austere, undecorated
Antonym: adorned, fancy, ornate
Further Information
- Originated from the Old Latin word *un + adornare* meaning "not" + "equip or furnish."
- **Unadorned** may also imply "unsophisticated."

unanimous: [yoo-NAN-uh-muh s] Adjective
Of one mind; in complete agreement.
Characterized by or showing complete agreement.

- The president won by a **unanimous** vote because of his promising manifesto.
- The class made a **unanimous** decision to have a Halloween party.

Synonym: uncontested, consistent, solid, unified, united
Antonym: divided, split
Further Information
- Originated from the Latin word *unus + animus* meaning "one" + "mind."
- **Unanimous** is usually misspelled as **unanimuous** which is not a word.

undecorated: [uhn-DEK-uh-rey-tid] Adjective
Ordinary or plain.

- The park is generally **undecorated** on any regular day.
- She likes **undecorated** furniture that goes along with her simple living room.

Synonym: simple, unadorned, vanilla, classic, clean
Antonym: decorated, adorned
Further Information
- Originated from the Latin word *un + decoratus* meaning "not" + "to decorate or adorn."
- In Military, **undecorated** means "not honored with an award."
- Undecorated and unadorned can be used interchangeably, though undecorated/decorated is used more commonly.

undergo: [uhn-der-GOH] Verb
To be subjected to; experience.
To endure; sustain.

- Wilma will **undergo** a minor surgery tomorrow.
- He will **undergo** two interviews to get the job that he wants.

Synonym: bear, endure, experience, have, see
Antonym: discontinue, refuse, surrender
Further Information
- Originated from the Old English word *undergan* meaning "undermine."
- To **bear** evokes a stronger emotion than to **undergo**.

undermine: [uhn-der-MAHYN] Verb
To injure or destroy especially gradually.
To attack by indirect, secret, or underhand means.

- Father had to cut down the tree outside because it was starting to **undermine** the foundation of the house.
- During a debate, one strategy is to **undermine** the confidence of your opponent.

Synonym: weaken, blunt, cripple, erode, frustrate
Antonym: aid, assist, build, construct, create
Further Information
- Originated from the Old English word *under + mine* meaning "beneath" + "pit or tunnel."
- **Undermine** is less direct than **cripple** or **weaken**.

undulate: [UHN-dyuh-leyt] for Verb/Adjective
To move with a sinuous or wavelike motion. (v.)
Having a wavelike or rippled form, surface, edge, etc. (adj.)

- The wheat field seems to **undulate** when the wind is blowing. (v.)
- The leaves look like they have an **undulated** margin. (adj.)

Synonym: billow, wave, flow, oscillate, ripple
Antonym: flat, steady
Further Information
- Originated from the Latin word *unda* meaning "a wave."
- **Undulate** implies a slower movement than **ripple**.

unimposing: [uhn-im-POH-zing] Adjective
Not grand or impressive in appearance.

- The celebrity looks **unimposing** in real life.
- His **unimposing** behavior makes him more approachable.

Synonym: unassuming, insignificant, considerate, humble
Antonym: arrogant, flashy, important
Further Information
- Originated from the 17th century word *un + impose* meaning "not" + "impressive."
- **UnImposing** implies "regular and approachable."

unique: [yoo-NEEK] Adjective/Noun
Existing as the only one or as the sole example. (adj.)
The embodiment of unique characteristics. (n.)

- His **unique** look makes him perfect for theater and show business. (adj.)
- We are looking for something **unique** among the flowers. (n.)

Synonym: alone, singular, different, exclusive, particular, special, distinctive
Antonym: common, normal, ordinary, regular, usual
Further Information
- Originated from the Latin word *unus* meaning "one."
- **Unique** means "being one of a kind" while **distinct** means "noticeable."

uproar: [UHP-rawr] Noun
A state of violent and noisy disturbance, as of a multitude.

- An **uproar** among the crowd was heard after the announcement.
- Be careful with such secrets or there will be an **uproar**.

Synonym: commotion, bickering, brawl, chaos, clamor
Antonym: calm, harmony, order, peace
Further Information
- Originated from the Middle Dutch *op + roer* meaning "up" + "confusion."
- **Uproar** may also mean "a loud and impassioned noise or disturbance."

vandal: [VAN-dl] Noun
A person who wilfully or ignorantly destroys or mars something beautiful or valuable.

- The **vandal** is being chased by the police.
- **Vandals** often paint over walls and pavements.

Synonym: despoiler, destroyer, hoodlum
Antonym: none
Further Information
- Originated from the *Vandals*, a name of a Germanic tribe.
- A **vandal** implies someone who commits something illegal.

REVIEW EXERCISE 41

Match the word with its synonym.

___	1.	trite	a.	wobble
___	2.	trough	b.	gutter
___	3.	unadorned	c.	hoodlum
___	4.	unanimous	d.	uncontested
___	5.	undecorated	e.	clamor
___	6.	undergo	f.	unassuming
___	7.	undermine	g.	weaken
___	8.	undulate	h.	endure
___	9.	unimposing	i.	banal
___	10.	unique	j.	simple
___	11.	uproar	k.	plain
___	12.	vandal	l.	distinctive

From the words above, fill in the blanks with the most appropriate word. The word form may need changing.

1. We dug a _____ to redirect the water and avoid getting flooded.

2. The house was plain and _____ when they purchased it.

3. No leader wants to be _____ by his subordinate.

4. The Christmas tree is still _____ a few days into the holidays.

5. The ship begins to _____ at the beginning of the storm.

6. The _____ building is designed using simple elements and lines.

7. Properties were destroyed by _____ during the riot.

8. People's thumbprints are _____ which is perfect for identification.

9. It is normal to _____ one or more interviews when you apply for a job.

10. The courtroom was in an _____ after the controversial decision was

    announced.

11. The song is filled with stereotypes and _____ ideas.

12. He was hoping for a _____ support for his leadership.

WORD SET 42

variable: [VAIR-ee-uh-buh l] Adjective/Noun
Liable to change. (adj.)
Something that may vary or change. (n.)

- The weather is highly **variable** making it difficult to plan the trip. (adj.)
- It is difficult to make predictions, as there are many **variables** involved. (n.)

Synonym: changing, fluctuating, volatile, changeable, varying
Antonym: stable, invariable
Further Information
- Originated from the Late Latin word *variare* meaning "to change."
- In Mathematics, a **variable** is "a quantity or function that may assume any given value or set of values."

venal: [VEEN-l] Adjective
Willing to sell one's influence, especially in return for a bribe.
Willing to do dishonest things in return for money.

- The **venal** mayor was caught accepting bribes.
- Elected politicians carry the trust of the people and should never be **venal.**

Synonym: bribable, corruptible, amoral, corrupt, crooked
Antonym: ethical, good, honest, moral, noble
Further Information
- Originated from the Latin word *venum* meaning "thing for sale."
- Its noun form **venality** is considered "a vice associated with being bribable."

veteran: [VET-er-uh n] Noun/Adjective
A person who has had long service or experience in an occupation, office, or the like. (n.)
Experienced through long service or practice. (adj.)

- Sam is considered a **veteran** in the field of sales. (n.)
- The world war **veteran** now works as a psychologist. (adj.)

Synonym: experienced, skilled, trained
Antonym: unskilled, amateur
Further Information
- Originated from the Latin word meaning *vetus* meaning "old."
- **Veteran** is also a common term for "soldiers who served."

vex: [veks] Verb
To irritate or annoy.
To foment trouble or cause worry.

- George sometimes would make the effort to **vex** me with his small problems.
- Lack of money **vexes** many people.

Synonym: distress, afflict, agitate, annoy, displease
Antonym: aid, appease, calm, comfort, delight
Further Information
- Originated from the Latin word *vexare* meaning "shake or disturb."
- **Vex** may also be used in Computer Science which refers to a coding scheme in digital circuits, as in VEX prefix (from "vector extension").

vigilance: [VIJ-uh-luh ns] Noun
The fact, quality, or state of keeping a careful watch for danger/difficulties.

- The **vigilance** of the police during emergencies is admirable.
- The lack of **vigilance** in the neighborhood made it vulnerable to thieves.

Synonym: carefulness, alertness, caution, diligence, surveillance
Antonym: indifference, neglect
Further Information
- Originated from the Latin word *vigilare* meaning "keep awake."
- **Vigilance** is a "state of awareness" while **focus** is "putting concentration towards a specific thing/task."

vile: [vahyl] Adjective
Highly offensive, unpleasant or objectionable.
Morally debased, depraved or despicable.

- Johnny sometimes displays a **vile** humor which other people don't like.
- There's a **vile** odor coming out of the laboratory, probably caused by chemicals.

Synonym: offensive, horrible, appalling, contemptible, depraved
Antonym: agreeable, attractive, comforting, decent, desirous
Further Information
- Originated from the Latin word *villis* meaning "cheap or base."
- Should not be confused with **vial**, also pronounced similarly, which means "a small container, as of glass, for holding liquids."

vindictive: [vin-DIK-tiv] Adjective
Disposed or inclined to revenge.
Proceeding from or showing a revengeful spirit.

- He is not a **vindictive** person and tends to forgive people easily.
- "Eye for an eye" is a **vindictive** attitude that often leads to trouble.

Synonym: hateful, revengeful, cruel, malicious, merciless
Antonym: compassionate, considerate, forgiving, gentle, giving
Further Information
- Originated from the Latin word *vindicta + ive* meaning "revenge" + adjectival suffix for verbs.
- **Vindictive** tends to imply that a person is being petty, while **vengeful** implies righteous anger.

vine: [vahyn] Noun
Any plant having a long, slender stem that trails or creeps on the ground or climbs by winding itself about a support or holding fast with tendrils or claspers.

- The **vines** I planted in the garden are growing nicely.
- Grapes grow on **vines** commonly cultivated in wineries.

Synonym: creeper
Antonym: none
Further Information
- Originated from the Latin word *vinum* meaning "wine."
- A related idiom **grapevine** means "an informal source of information such as gossip."

virulent: [VIR-yuh-luh nt] Adjective
Actively poisonous.
Intensely bitter, spiteful, or malicious.

- A **virulent** strain of influenza is sweeping through the country and has caused many casualties.
- His opponent's **virulent** attacks are not effective, as he just ignores them.

Synonym: poisonous, lethal, deadly, destructive, fatal
Antonym: harmless, healthful, helpful, wholesome
Further Information
- Originated from the Latin word *virus* meaning "poison."
- In Medicine, **virulent** means "highly effective or malignant."

visor: [VAHY-zer] Noun
A movable part of a helmet that can be pulled down to cover the face.
A screen for protecting the eyes from direct sunlight especially in vehicles.
The projecting front brim of a cap.

- The baseball cap's **visor** is obscuring his face and hides his identity.
- The plastic safety helmet had a transparent **visor**.

Synonym: bill, brim, screen
Antonym: none
Further Information
- Originated from the Latin word *visus* meaning "a look or vision."
- **Visor** may also be spelled **vizor**.

vociferous: [voh-SIF-er-uh s] Adjective
Expressing loudly and forcefully.
Characterized by vehemence, clamor, or noisiness.

- Everyone can hear the **vociferous** protests outside the office building.
- The boss is a **vociferous** man who loudly expresses his thoughts.

Synonym: loud, insistent, boisterous, clamorous, noisy
Antonym: low, quiet, silent, soft
Further Information
- Originated from the Latin word *vox + ferre* meaning "voice" + "to carry."
- **Vociferous** is sometimes misspelled as **vociferuous** which is not a word.

volatile: [VOL-uh-tahyl] Adjective
(Of a substance) Easily evaporated at normal temperature.
Rapidly changeable; mercurial.

- The political climate today is very **volatile** and unstable.
- Firemen are experts in handling **volatile** situations during emergencies.

Synonym: explosive, changeable, capricious, vaporous
Antonym: certain, constant, definite, dependable, reliable
Further Information
- Originated from the Latin word *volare* meaning "to fly."
- In Computer Science, **volatile** is related to "a storage that does not retain data when there's no electricity, such as RAM."

REVIEW EXERCISE 42

Match the word with its synonym.

___	1.	variable	a.	varying
___	2.	venal	b.	experienced
___	3.	veteran	c.	revengeful
___	4.	vex	d.	horrible
___	5.	vigilance	e.	insistent
___	6.	vile	f.	annoy
___	7.	vindictive	g.	changeable
___	8.	vine	h.	creeper
___	9.	virulent	i.	poisonous
___	10.	visor	j.	caution
___	11.	vociferous	k.	bribable
___	12.	volatile	l.	screen

From the words above, fill in the blanks with the most appropriate word. The word form may need changing.

1. The motor-cyclist raised his _____ to take a better look.

2. Dan's _____ support for the party was recognized by the leadership.

3. It's _____ me to think that some people are gossiping about me, behind my back.

4. Do not anger him as he has a _____ temper and can become violent.

5. The _____ magistrate was caught and punished by the court.

6. The security staff's _____prevented the theft.

7. The _____ heart surgeon was sought by hospitals all over the world.

8. There is an overgrown _____ outside the house that needs trimming.

9. Controversial celebrities sometimes face _____ attacks by the media.

10. The sugar content in different foods is very _____.

11. May is in a _____ mood today because her pet died.

12. The _____ man seeks revenge against his enemies.

WORD SET 43

vulgar: [VUHL-ger] Adjective
Characterized by ignorance of or lack of good breeding or taste.
Lacking in distinction, aesthetic value, or charm.

- Everyone looked at him when he uttered those **vulgar** words.
- **Vulgar** behavior is not welcome in the playing field.

Synonym: rude, offensive, boorish, coarse, crude
Antonym: chaste, clean, decent, gentle, moral
Further Information
- Originated from the Latin word *vulgus* meaning "common people."
- **Vulgar** generally implies "offensive or rude" while **profane** implies "offense to religious beliefs."

waft: [wahft] Verb/Noun
To carry lightly and smoothly through the air or over water. (v.)
A sound, odor, etc., faintly perceived. (n.)

- The delicious smell of freshly baked cookies **wafted** in the garden. (v.)
- He smelled a **waft** of perfume that was so familiar. (n.)

Synonym: carry, drift, float, whiff
Antonym: hold, keep
Further Information
- Originated from the Dutch word *wachten* meaning "to guard."
- **Waft** implies "something carried through the air" while **whiff** implies "the action of smelling."

waive: [weyv] Verb
To refrain from claiming or insisting on.
To refrain from demanding compliance with.

- The bank will **waive** all the extra fees so I can pay my loans.
- Let's **waive** the formalities and get right down to business.

Synonym: give up, let go, abandon, defer, forgo
Antonym: approve, continue, deny, do, expedite
Further Information
- Originated from the Old French word *gaiver* meaning "allow to become a waif or abandon."
- Should not be confused with **wave** which is "a disturbance on the surface of a liquid body."

walkout: [WAWK-out] Noun/Adjective
The act of leaving or being absent from a meeting. (n.)
Having a doorway that gives direct access to the outdoors. (adj.)

- The students are planning a **walkout** as a form of protest. (n.)
- My father is building a **walkout** basement. (adj.)

Synonym: demonstrate, manifest, protest
Antonym: lose, conceal
Further Information
- First used in the 1800s to mean "a strike."
- **Walkout** can also be spelled as **walk-out**.

wane: [weyn] Verb/ Noun
To decrease in strength, intensity, etc. (v.)
A gradual decrease or decline in strength, intensity, power, etc. (n.)

- Winter is about to **wane** and we can see traces of spring. (v.)
- It is interesting to see and study the moonlight's **wane**. (n.)

Synonym: diminish, lessen, abate, decrease, dim
Antonym: brighten, develop, enhance, enlarge, expand, wax
Further Information
- Originated from the Old English word *wanian* meaning "make or become smaller gradually."
- Should not be confused with **wean** meaning "to withdraw from some object, habit, form of enjoyment."
- **Waxing and Waning** is usually used to represent the phases of the moon.

weary: [WEER-ee] Adjective/Verb
Physically or mentally exhausted by hard work, exertion, strain, etc. (adj.)
To make or become weary. (v.)

- His **weary** smile tells me it's time to go home. (adj.)
- The long hours at work have made everyone **weary**. (v.)

Synonym: tired, bored, disgusted, exhausted, fatigued
Antonym: animated, energetic, fresh, lively, refreshed
Further Information
- Originated from the Old English word *werig/wergian* meaning "tired or miserable."
- Should not be confused with **wary** meaning "being watchful."

woven: [WOH-vuh n] Verb
To interlace (threads, yarns, strips, fibrous material, etc.) so as to form a fabric or material.
To form by combining various elements or details into a connected whole.

- The **woven** basket looks sturdy enough to hold these apples.
- Adam's **woven** lies were easily unraveled on cross-questioning.

Synonym: spun, interlaced, interlinked, intertwined, interwoven
Antonym: none
Further Information
- Originated from the Old English word *wefan* meaning "to weave or interlace."
- **Woven** is often used to describe fabrics or clothes.

writhe: [rahyth] Verb
To twist the body about, or squirm, as in pain, violent effort, etc.
Respond with great emotional or physical discomfort.

- She was in so much pain that she began to **writhe** on the floor.
- He bit his lip, **writhing** in suppressed fury.

Synonym: contort, recoil, squirm, wiggle, wince, agonize
Antonym: straighten
Further Information
- Originated from the Proto-Germanic word *writhanan* meaning "to turn or bend."
- Should not be confused with **wraith** which means "an apparition of a living person supposed to portend his or her death."

yearn: [yurn] Verb
To have an earnest or strong desire.
To feel tenderness.

- Ken **yearns** for a quick time off from his busy schedule.
- Sometimes he **yearns** for a tub of ice cream late at night.

Synonym: ache, chafe, covert, crave, hanker
Antonym: abjure, dislike, hate
Further Information
- Originated from the Old English word *giernan* meaning "to strive or be eager."
- Should not be confused with **yarn** which is "a thread made of natural or synthetic fibers and used for knitting and weaving" or "(informal) a long implausible story."

zenith: [ZEN-ith] Noun
The apex point or summit.
The time at which something is most powerful or successful.

- We are approaching the **zenith** of our technological innovation.
- The sun is now near its **zenith**.

Synonym: top, acme, altitude, apex, apogee
Antonym: base, bottom, depth
Further Information
- Originated from the Arabic phrase *samt ar-ras* meaning "the way over the head."
- **Zenith** typically refers to celestial bodies.

REVIEW EXERCISE 43

Match the word with its synonym.

___	1. vulgar	a.	defer
___	2. waft	b.	interlaced
___	3. waive	c.	squirm
___	4. walkout	d.	lessen
___	5. wane	e.	ache
___	6. weary	f.	drift
___	7. woven	g.	rude
___	8. writhe	h.	protest
___	9. yearn	i.	bored
___	10. zenith	j.	apex

From the words above, fill in the blanks with the most appropriate word. The word form may need changing.

1. The captive monkey _____ for freedom after years in the cage.

2. The offensive remark made her _____ in embarrassment.

3. The film is _____ and a tad offensive.

4. His interest in Maths _____ when he began training as an artist.

5. Some museums _____ their entrance fees for students.

6. The _____ traveler arrived at the hotel.

7. Being the company CEO is the _____ of his career.

8. A _____ is a form of peaceful protest commonly used by politicians.

9. The beautiful melody _____ through the concert hall.

10. Plot twists were _____ into the novel's plot making it very interesting.

Review Exercises Solutions

Review Exercise 1

Matching
1. d
2. f
3. a
4. l
5. e
6. b
7. k
8. c
9. j
10. g
11. i
12. h

Fill in the Blanks
1. admired
2. abrasive
3. abide
4. abdicates
5. aberration
6. activism
7. admonish
8. abhorrent
9. accredited
10. abundance
11. abstain
12. abysmal

Review Exercise 2

Matching
1. b
2. d
3. g
4. h
5. e
6. a
7. l
8. k
9. c
10. f
11. j
12. i

Fill in the Blanks
1. affluent
2. ailment
3. adroit
4. ancestral
5. aggregate
6. amenable
7. alternate
8. affirmed
9. amassed
10. anomaly
11. annotated
12. affable

Review Exercise 3

Matching
1. h
2. k
3. g
4. i
5. f
6. c
7. d
8. a
9. l
10. b
11. e
12. j

Fill in the Blanks
1. arrogant
2. aromatic
3. apprehensive
4. articulate
5. artillery
6. appalling
7. apathetic
8. appreciable
9. apex
10. ascendant
11. arbitrary
12. apparent

Review Exercise 4

Matching

1. g
2. j
3. b
4. k
5. f
6. l
7. h
8. d
9. i
10. c
11. e
12. a

Fill in the Blanks

1. belated
2. barometer
3. assimilate
4. awe
5. assess
6. austerity
7. astounded
8. benevolent
9. augments
10. astute
11. avid
12. bellowing

Review Exercise 5

Matching

1. d
2. l
3. c
4. h
5. g
6. i
7. a
8. f
9. b
10. J
11. e
12. k

Fill in the Blanks

1. berth
2. callous
3. caustic
4. brooch
5. billiards
6. bolster
7. caricature
8. boon
9. cacophony
10. bystanders
11. cavity
12. bilinguals

Review Exercise 6

Matching

1. d
2. c
3. a
4. k
5. g
6. b
7. h
8. l
9. i
10. f
11. j
12. e

Fill in the Blanks

1. cellar
2. chastised
3. celebrated
4. coalesced
5. coddling
6. clandestine
7. cohabit
8. chronic
9. clamor
10. chalet
11. cleft
12. ceded

Review Exercise 7

Matching
1. h
2. e
3. l
4. j
5. f
6. k
7. d
8. c
9. g
10. a
11. b
12. i

Fill in the Blanks
1. coils
2. colluded
3. commerce
4. complacent
5. complement
6. compliant
7. composed
8. compromise
9. conceited
10. concise
11. concocted
12. coherence

Review Exercise 8

Matching
1. h
2. f
3. i
4. l
5. d
6. k
7. c
8. a
9. e
10. b
11. g
12. j

Fill in the Blanks
1. conscientious
2. congestion
3. contemptible
4. confront
5. consented
6. consolidated
7. condolences
8. concur
9. contentious
10. contemporary
11. conspiracy
12. confectionery

Review Exercise 9

Matching
1. e
2. j
3. h
4. i
5. k
6. b
7. f
8. d
9. g
10. l
11. a
12. c

Fill in the Blanks
1. cordial
2. contrived
3. conversant
4. coping
5. convent
6. contrary
7. corroborates
8. counter
9. convey
10. convivial
11. copious
12. convened

Review Exercise 10

Matching

1. e
2. d
3. i
4. j
5. h
6. g
7. b
8. a
9. k
10. c
11. f
12. l

Fill in the Blanks

1. craft
2. crease
3. cumulate
4. courier
5. craven
6. dally
7. dearth
8. culminated
9. crevice
10. crude
11. creche
12. credulous

Review Exercise 11

Matching

1. g
2. f
3. b
4. h
5. a
6. k
7. i
8. e
9. j
10. d
11. c
12. l

Fill in the Blanks

1. demoted
2. delirious
3. demeaned
4. demeanor
5. deflected
6. demise
7. delinquent
8. decorum
9. denoted
10. deliberate
11. debasing
12. decisive

Review Exercise 12

Matching

1. k
2. d
3. e
4. i
5. h
6. l
7. b
8. a
9. g
10. f
11. j
12. c

Fill in the Blanks

1. depleted
2. destitute
3. derivative
4. derive
5. despicable
6. devious
7. detrimental
8. deterrents
9. deplorable
10. desist
11. deviated
12. depicts

Review Exercise 13

Matching
1. i
2. c
3. k
4. g
5. d
6. l
7. e
8. f
9. j
10. h
11. a
12. b

Fill in the Blanks
1. devout
2. diligent
3. dialects
4. diplomatic
5. diminutive
6. disdain
7. discarded
8. devoid
9. disadvantaged
10. dilate
11. dingy
12. dichotomy

Review Exercise 14

Matching
1. f
2. b
3. c
4. g
5. a
6. l
7. k
8. e
9. j
10. h
11. i
12. d

Fill in the Blanks
1. disowned
2. dissecting
3. disingenuous
4. disembark
5. disinclination
6. domestic
7. divulged
8. dogmatic
9. divinity
10. distinguished
11. doleful
12. disparage

Review Exercise 15

Matching
1. k
2. d
3. c
4. g
5. l
6. a
7. j
8. i
9. f
10. e
11. h
12. b

Fill in the Blanks
1. eloquence
2. draft
3. earnest
4. effervescent
5. ebb
6. drab
7. drenched
8. dwindled
9. embargo
10. economy
11. eerie
12. elegant

Review Exercise 16

Matching

1. h
2. g
3. k
4. d
5. e
6. b
7. j
8. a
9. i
10. l
11. f
12. c

Fill in the Blanks

1. embezzling
2. endorse
3. engulfed
4. empathetic
5. enduring
6. enmity
7. enthralling
8. engender
9. embellished
10. encrypt
11. enthusiastic
12. ensuing

Review Exercise 17

Matching

1. j
2. k
3. c
4. a
5. i
6. e
7. g
8. d
9. b
10. f
11. h
12. l

Fill in the Blanks

1. equine
2. erratic
3. err
4. excavate
5. equivocal
6. epoch
7. evinced
8. enumerate
9. exacerbate
10. exonerated
11. ethnic
12. errands

Review Exercise 18

Matching

1. c
2. k
3. e
4. h
5. j
6. a
7. b
8. f
9. l
10. i
11. d
12. g

Fill in the Blanks

1. extravagant
2. fanatic
3. fallacious
4. fastidious
5. exuberance
6. expeditious
7. fits
8. extrapolate
9. exorbitant
10. fissure
11. fanatical
12. extensive

Review Exercise 19

Matching
1. f
2. h
3. c
4. a
5. g
6. i
7. j
8. e
9. k
10. b
11. d

Fill in the Blanks
1. foliage
2. flannel
3. flourish
4. forthright
5. flowery
6. forgery
7. flirtatious
8. florists
9. flamboyant
10. frivolous
11. fortified
12. forlorn

Review Exercise 20

Matching
1. f
2. i
3. h
4. j
5. a
6. k
7. e
8. l
9. b
10. d
11. c
12. g

Fill in the Blanks
1. gregarious
2. glade
3. fundamental
4. glib
5. gnashed
6. gouged
7. ghastly
8. garish
9. governor
10. garments
11. futile
12. glut

Review Exercise 21

Matching
1. i
2. g
3. b
4. j
5. a
6. e
7. d
8. k
9. l
10. c
11. h
12. f

Fill in the Blanks
1. impending
2. impenetrable
3. grudging
4. humid
5. hackneyed
6. grovel
7. guile
8. hallowed
9. humble
10. hoist
11. hesitant
12. horrific

Review Exercise 22

Matching

1. a
2. f
3. b
4. j
5. k
6. c
7. d
8. e
9. h
10. g
11. i
12. l

Fill in the Blanks

1. inattentive
2. indeterminate
3. imperative
4. imperious
5. impish
6. indispensable
7. inadvertently
8. implicated
9. impetuous
10. indulge
11. industrious
12. implored

Review Exercise 23

Matching

1. g
2. c
3. h
4. b
5. a
6. f
7. k
8. e
9. i
10. d
11. j
12. l

Fill in the Blanks

1. innocuous
2. inevitable
3. integrity
4. intermittently
5. intervals
6. inherent
7. inedible
8. integrate
9. invigorated
10. insulate
11. introverted
12. insurmountable

Review Exercise 24

Matching

1. j
2. e
3. b
4. l
5. d
6. k
7. i
8. g
9. h
10. a
11. f
12. c

Fill in the Blanks

1. ire
2. lackluster
3. landmark
4. juxtaposed
5. invoked
6. languid
7. jibe
8. jeered
9. languished
10. jaunt
11. jeopardy
12. jaded

Review Exercise 25

Matching
1. b
2. g
3. h
4. j
5. c
6. k
7. i
8. a
9. e
10. f
11. l
12. d

Fill in the Blanks
1. lethargic
2. maligned
3. lurid
4. lodging
5. liveliness
6. malicious
7. liberating
8. lout
9. lucrative
10. lauded
11. liberated
12. magistrate

Review Exercise 26

Matching
1. g
2. k
3. l
4. d
5. f
6. a
7. i
8. c
9. h
10. j
11. b
12. e

Fill in the Blanks
1. minuscule
2. momentous
3. marquee
4. meritorious
5. mews
6. maltreat
7. mollified
8. mitigate
9. missionaries
10. merciless
11. memorandum
12. meticulous

Review Exercise 27

Matching
1. e
2. f
3. i
4. g
5. k
6. l
7. a
8. d
9. b
10. c
11. j
12. h

Fill in the Blanks
1. navel
2. motivating
3. muffled
4. necessity
5. monotonous
6. monuments
7. moult
8. nebulous
9. naval
10. mundane
11. mound
12. negated

Review Exercise 28

Matching
1. k
2. d
3. e
4. j
5. c
6. a
7. i
8. f
9. b
10. h
11. l
12. g

Fill in the Blanks
1. obesity
2. obstinate
3. oblivious
4. oasis
5. obnoxious
6. obliged
7. novice
8. obligatory
9. obtrusive
10. nonsensical
11. notorious
12. nurturing

Review Exercise 29

Matching
1. i
2. l
3. j
4. f
5. e
6. h
7. a
8. d
9. k
10. b
11. c
12. g

Fill in the Blanks
1. occupation
2. padlock
3. parched
4. orators
5. palatial
6. oscillate
7. partisan
8. optimal
9. odious
10. orchestrated
11. peculiar
12. parry

Review Exercise 30

Matching
1. g
2. b
3. a
4. c
5. d
6. e
7. l
8. i
9. j
10. h
11. k
12. f

Fill in the Blanks
1. perpetuate
2. permeated
3. perceptive
4. peripheral
5. pensive
6. pervasive
7. perception
8. pious
9. philanthropy
10. pendant
11. petty
12. pinnacle

Review Exercise 31

Matching
1. g
2. e
3. a
4. h
5. i
6. d
7. k
8. l
9. j
10. b
11. c
12. f

Fill in the Blanks
1. poverty
2. podcasts
3. pliers
4. piqued
5. platonic
6. preamble
7. pored
8. pivotal
9. populous
10. placate
11. pliable
12. postponed

Review Exercise 32

Matching
1. j
2. f
3. e
4. a
5. b
6. l
7. h
8. i
9. k
10. c
11. d
12. g

Fill in the Blanks
1. perseverance
2. prepay
3. prospective
4. pretentious
5. pulverized
6. preliminary
7. profligate
8. pungent
9. proposal
10. prosperous
11. proficient
12. predicament

Review Exercise 33

Matching
1. c
2. j
3. l
4. h
5. d
6. i
7. a
8. b
9. g
10. e
11. k
12. f

Fill in the Blanks
1. quarantined
2. regal
3. realm
4. reconcile
5. refrain
6. ransacked
7. refuted
8. quart
9. rectify
10. quilt
11. quaint
12. recapitulate

Review Exercise 34

Matching

1. k
2. c
3. l
4. i
5. d
6. b
7. f
8. a
9. e
10. j
11. g
12. h

Fill in the Blanks

1. resistant
2. reproached
3. registration
4. retreat
5. replete
6. renegade
7. retracted
8. reprieve
9. restricted
10. repealed
11. retaliate
12. residue

Review Exercise 35

Matching

1. l
2. a
3. e
4. f
5. b
6. g
7. h
8. k
9. j
10. c
11. d
12. i

Fill in the Blanks

1. savvy
2. scant
3. ruthless
4. reverts
5. sanitary
6. riveting
7. scarcity
8. salient
9. righteously
10. ridge
11. sanctioned
12. satiated

Review Exercise 36

Matching

1. e
2. a
3. k
4. b
5. h
6. c
7. f
8. d
9. j
10. i
11. g
12. l

Fill in the Blanks

1. shambles
2. scrupulous
3. sincere
4. scornful
5. severed
6. shrill
7. segregation
8. scorn
9. self-esteem
10. shun
11. serpent
12. shrewd

Review Exercise 37

Matching

1. c
2. h
3. g
4. k
5. l
6. e
7. f
8. a
9. b
10. d
11. i
12. j

Fill in the Blanks

1. sodden
2. sophisticated
3. sneering
4. sinuous
5. solace
6. sparse
7. spearhead
8. solvent
9. smother
10. sole
11. spanner
12. snivelling

Review Exercise 38

Matching

1. i
2. f
3. d
4. j
5. k
6. h
7. c
8. g
9. b
10. l
11. e
12. a

Fill in the Blanks

1. strumming
2. stowaway
3. spurned
4. squander
5. springboard
6. spoofs
7. sporadic
8. sphere
9. stampede
10. stethoscope
11. spire
12. squabble

Review Exercise 39

Matching

1. i
2. d
3. c
4. a
5. g
6. h
7. e
8. k
9. l
10. f
11. b
12. j

Fill in the Blanks

1. sugarcoating
2. subsided
3. tarnish
4. synthetic
5. sycophants
6. succulent
7. tactful
8. surplus
9. suppressed
10. swivelled
11. synthesis
12. tantalized

Review Exercise 40

Matching
1. j
2. d
3. c
4. k
5. a
6. b
7. h
8. e
9. i
10. g
11. f
12. l

Fill in the Blanks
1. thriving
2. tentative
3. terse
4. trinkets
5. temperate
6. tempestuous
7. thistle
8. thaw
9. tiller
10. tarnished
11. tournament
12. towbar

Review Exercise 41

Matching
1. i
2. b
3. k (or j)
4. d
5. j (or k)
6. h
7. g
8. a
9. f
10. l
11. e
12. c

Fill in the Blanks
1. trough
2. unadorned
3. undermined
4. undecorated
5. undulate
6. unimposing
7. vandals
8. unique
9. undergo
10. uproar
11. trite
12. unanimous

Review Exercise 42

Matching
1. a
2. k
3. b
4. f
5. j
6. d
7. c
8. h
9. i
10. l
11. e
12. g

Fill in the Blanks
1. visor
2. vociferous
3. vexing
4. volatile
5. venal
6. vigilance
7. veteran
8. vine
9. virulent
10. variable
11. vile
12. vindictive

Review Exercise 43

Matching

1. g
2. f
3. a
4. h
5. d
6. i
7. b
8. c
9. e
10. j

Fill in the Blanks

1. yearns
2. writhe
3. vulgar
4. waned
5. waive
6. weary
7. zenith
8. walkout
9. wafted
10. woven

Word List

abdicate
aberration
abhorrent
abide
abrasive
abstain
abundance
abysmal
accredited
activism
admirer
admonish
adroit
affable
affirm
affluent
aggregate
ailment
alternate
amass
amenable
ancestral
annotate
anomaly
apathetic
apex
appalling
apparent
appreciable
apprehensive
arbitrary
aromatic
arrogant
articulate
artillery
ascendant
assess
assimilate
astound
astute
astute
augment
austerity
avid
awe
barometer

belated
bellow
benevolent
berth
bilingual
billiards
bolster
boon
brooch
bystander
cacophony
callous
caricature
caustic
cavity
cede
celebrated
cellars
chalet
chastise
chronic
clamor
clandestine
cleft
coalesce
coddle
cohabit
coherence
coil
collude
commerce
complacent
complement
compliant
composed
compromise
conceited
concise
concoct
concur
condolence
confectionery
confront
congestion
conscientious
consent

consolidate
conspiracy
contemporary
contemptible
contentious
contrary
contrived
convene
convent
conversant
convey
convivial
cope
copious
cordial
corroborate
counter
courier
craft
craven
crease
creche
credulous
crevices
crude
culminate
cumulate
dally
dearth
debase
decisive
decorum
deflect
deliberate
delinquent
delirious
demean
demeanor
demise
demote
demure
denote
depict
depleted
deplorable
derivative

derive
desist
despicable
destitute
deterrent
detrimental
deviate
devious
devoid
devout
dialect
dichotomy
dilate
diligent
diminutive
dingy
diplomatic
disadvantaged
discard
disdain
disembark
disinclination
disingenuous
disown
disparage
dissect
distinguished
divinity
divulge
dogmatic
doleful
domestic
drab
draft
drench
dwindle
earnest
ebb
economy
eerie
effervescent
elegant
eloquence
embargo
embellish
embezzle
empathetic
encrypt

endorse
enduring
engender
engulfed
enmity
ensuing
enthralling
enthusiastic
enumerate
epoch
equine
equivocal
err
errand
erratic
ethnic
evince
exacerbate
excavate
exonerate
exorbitant
expeditious
extensive
extrapolate
extravagant
exuberance
fallacious
fanatic
fanatical
fastidious
fissure
fits
flamboyant
flannel
flirtatious
florist
flourish
flowery
foliage
forgery
forlorn
forthright
fortified
frivolous
fundamental
futile
garish
garment

ghastly
glade
glib
glut
gnashed
gouged
governor
gregarious
grovel
grudging
guile
hackneyed
hallowed
hesitant
hoist
horrific
humble
humid
impending
impenetrable
imperative
imperious
impetuous
impish
implicate
implore
inadvertent
inattentive
indeterminate
indispensable
indulge
industrious
inedible
inevitable
inherent
innocuous
insulate
insurmountable
integrate
integrity
intermittently
interval
introvert
invigorated
invoke
ire
jaded
jaunt

jeer
jeopardy
jibe
juxtaposed
lackluster
landmark
languid
languish
laud
lethargic
liberate
liberation
liveliness
lodging
lout
lucrative
lurid
magistrate
malicious
malign
maltreat
marquee
memorandum
merciless
meritorious
meticulous
mews
minuscule
missionary
mitigate
mollify
momentous
monotonous
monument
motivate
moult
mound
muffled
mundane
naval
navel
nebulous
nebulous
necessity
negate
nonsensical
notorious

novice
nurture
nurture
oasis
obese
obligatory
oblige
oblivious
obnoxious
obstinate
obtrusive
occupation
odious
optimal
orator
orchestrate
oscillate
padlock
palatial
parched
parry
partisan
peculiar
pendant
pensive
perception
perceptive
peripheral
permeate
perpetuate
pervasive
petty
philanthropy
pinnacle
pious
pique
pivotal
placate
platonic
pliable
pliers
podcast
populous
pore
postpone
poverty
preamble

predicament
preliminary
prepay
pretentious
proficient
profligate
proposal
prospective
prosper
prosperous
pulverize
pungent
quaint
quarantine
quart
quilt
ransack
realm
recapitulate
reconcile
rectify
refrain
refute
regal
registration
renegade
repealed
replete
reprieve
reproach
residue
resistant
restricted
retaliate
retract
retreat
revert
ridge
righteously
riveting
ruthless
salient
sanction
sanitary
satiated
savvy
scant

scarcity

scorn

scornful

scrupulous

segregation

self-esteem

serpent

severed

shambles

shrewd

shrill

shun

sincere

sinuous

smother

sneering

snivel

sodden

solace

sole

solvent

sophisticated

spanner

sparse

spearhead

sphere

spire

spoof

sporadically

springboard

spurn

squabble

squander

stampede

stethoscope

stowaway

strum

subside

succulent

sugar coat

suppress

surplus

swivel

sycophant

synthesis

synthetic

tactful

tantalize

tarnish

tarnished

temperate

tempestuous

tentative

terse

thaw

thistle

thriving

tiller

tournament

tow bar

trinket

trite

trough

unadorned

unanimous

undecorated

undergo

undermine

undulate

unimposing

unique

uproar

vandal

variable

venal

veteran

vex

vigilance

vile

vindictive

vine

virulent

visor

vociferous

volatile

vulgar

waft

waive

walkout

wane

weary

woven

writhe

yearn

zenith

Complimentary Audio Program

This book has helped *thousands* of 11+ students improve their score and we look forward to hearing your personal success story!

Please let us know how this book helped you, and as a special note of thanks for sharing your success story, we will give you our bestselling audio program;

"Double your Reading speed in 60 minutes" - **Audio Program**
This program will teach you how to actually double … triple – or even QUADRUPLE your reading speed and comprehension for SSAT & ISEE.
It will enable you to soak up complex information quickly without sacrificing comprehension.
You will learn why mastery of this simple core technique is all that you need to zip through your reading!

This is a complete program and you will get it with our compliments, at zero cost to you.

Simply go to the web page below, follow the simple instructions, and you will have the Audio Program with you within a few days.

https://99percentileprep.com/500ssatisee

Here is wishing you the best of luck with your learning!

PS: This book has undergone multiple rounds of thorough proof-reading.

In the unlikely case that you spot any errors in the book, kindly report them via a contact details in the web link above.

V1.1

Made in United States
Troutdale, OR
10/24/2024